Yours respectfully

Theobald Boehm.

Munich the 4th of March 1872.

THE FLUTE AND FLUTE-PLAYING

IN ACOUSTICAL, TECHNICAL,
AND ARTISTIC ASPECTS

by

THEOBALD BOEHM

Royal Bavarian Court-Musician

Translated by
DAYTON C. MILLER
With a new introduction by
SAMUEL BARON
Flutist, New York Woodwind Quintet and
New York Chamber Soloists

NEW YORK
DOVER PUBLICATIONS, INC.

This Dover edition, first published in 1964, is an unabridged and unaltered republication of the second revised and enlarged edition published by Dayton C. Miller in 1922.

This Dover edition also contains a new Introduction by Samuel Baron.

International Standard Book Number: 0-486-21259-9
Library of Congress Catalog Card Number: 64-15498

Manufactured in the United States of America
Dover Publications, Inc.
180 Varick Street
New York, N.Y. 10014

INTRODUCTION TO
THE DOVER EDITION

Theobald Boehm had a unique combination of skills. He was a master flutist, a master gold- and silversmith, and a keen student of physics and acoustics as they apply to the flute. The master flutist and musician realized what was lacking in the flute of his day: his ear was dissatisfied with the poor intonation, limited range and uneven tonal response of his chosen instrument. The keen student of physics and acoustics considered what might be the causes, what might be the improvements. And finally the mechanic, the man who could make things and make them work, created the forms that could realize his ideas.

All of this is known from history, and we flutists know it best of all, for we play on a Boehm flute virtually unchanged from his work bench of 1847 to the present day. There have been fine flute makers since, and many splendid flutes have been built, but the design, the proportions and the *theory* of the flute come from this book, which is as valid today as it ever was.

Reading Boehm's book is an absorbing experience in following the progress of an idea. But it is more than that, too. The view of the man himself is enlightening and endearing. He writes in a most objective style but he cannot conceal the mellowness of a hard-won wisdom. This wisdom is shared openly with all who are interested. It is the ideal attitude of the scientist who says, "We are all working to penetrate the unknown. My contribution may help someone else; it may throw some light on a seemingly unrelated problem; it may have an application that I don't think of.   Let anyone who is interested know my work!''

In addition there is an attitude about the old man that stamps him as a great teacher.   To Boehm, the creative man is the one who teaches *himself* something. It follows from this that he can teach others too. Notice the emphasis on the *rational* process and the *rational* ideal in the following words of Boehm:

> . . . for he alone is capable of carrying out a rational work, who can give a complete account of the why and wherefore of every detail from the conception to the completion. (*An Essay on the Construction of Flutes*)

This emphasis is carried through his work.

Boehm's respect for the practical and the pragmatic is very strong.   Again and again he finds the solution to his problem by trying many ways.   For example: how to determine the shortening of the tube necessary to give the chromatic intervals of the bottom octave. Boehm's solution:

> The simplest and shortest method is, naturally, successively to cut off from the lower end of the flute tube so much as will make the length of the air column correspond to each tone of the chromatic scale.   In order that these proportions might be accurately verified, I made a tube in which all the twelve tone sections could be taken off and again put together.   (*The Flute and Flute-Playing*, p. 25)

When he had accomplished this much he found that the placement of the tone holes did not exactly correspond to the cutting off of the tube, so he endeavored to find the relationship between the two systems:

> For the exact determination of these positions and the other tuning proportions, I had a flute made with movable holes, and was thus enabled to adjust all the tones higher or lower at pleasure.   (*The Flute and Flute-Playing*, p. 30)

At this point I ask the reader, just what is a flute with movable tone holes? To my unmechanical mind, such an ingenious gadget should win prizes for its inventor, but for Boehm it was merely a means to an end. It was a step along the way—he never mentions it again.

So we have here a very interesting man, one who had the patience and courage, not to mention the ingenuity, to see his work through "from the conception to the completion" even though he was going against the beliefs of his time.   For in Boehm's day musicians and instrument makers believed that the holes should be bored into the flute at points where the player's fingers could easily cover them.   This was considered to be common sense as well as "humanistic."   Boehm said, in effect, "Let us put the holes where they belong, according to science and the tempered scale.   If the fingers cannot reach them, let us use our brain to invent some system for controlling the opening and shutting of the tone holes."   This was uncommon sense, and humanistic on a higher plane.

A flutist of international reputation, he did not hesitate, at the age of thirty-eight, to redesign his own instrument, endangering, as he says,

> ... my facility in playing which had been acquired by twenty years of practice. (*The Flute and Flute-Playing*, p. 3)

And when the new instrument was not completely satisfactory to him, he did not shrink from taking two years for the study of physics and acoustics (at the age of fifty-two) and utilizing what he then learned to make still more drastic revisions in his design.   At no point did he allow himself to be swayed by the comments of his fellow professionals who might have said, "Look here! Aren't you really ruining the business for us? Our students are going to take this new flute, as you call it, and do better than we can—and we have given our lives to the flute!''

All who are interested in the flute should visit the Library of Congress in Washington, D.C., which houses the flute collection of Dayton C. Miller, translator and editor of this book. There on display are many of the best flutes of pre-Boehm days. What monstrosities of frustrated ingenuity are to be seen there! One maker devised a Rube Goldberg key to trill C♯ to D♯. Another figured out three ways to play F natural and built them all onto the instrument. A hodge-podge of keys and levers seems to grow in baroque profusion over the simple flute of Quantz—but to little avail. The instrument is still limited in range, still out of tune, and clumsy to play in the remote keys. By contrast, Boehm's flute, which put an end to this "let's add a key here and another there" mentality— how simple! how functional! how really well it plays!

How satisfying is the triumph of a rational work!

SAMUEL BARON

April, 1964.

Munich, August 6th, 1908

Dear Mr. Miller:—

I wish to express my, and my sister's, great pleasure and satisfaction for your labor of love, which you have undertaken in the good intention to honor my grandfather. For this we can be only very thankful to you; and I believe I express the sentiment of the whole family of my grandfather in giving you our approval of the publishing of your translation of his book: "Die Flöte und das Flötenspiel."

Yours very truly

Theobald Böhm

[The above is an extract from a personal letter; the original is written in English.]

PREFACE TO THE SECOND
ENGLISH EDITION

SHORTLY after the publication of the first English edition of "The Flute and Flute-Playing," the translator received a letter dated at Preston, Cuba, April 7, 1909, a portion of which is as follows:

"Dear Sir:—I saw the notice of your work on the Flute, and it interested me for I lived in Munich for three years (beginning May, 1871) and studied flute under Mr. Boehm. I also worked one winter (1872-73) in the shop with Mendler. At that time I translated Mr. Boehm's work on the flute, "Die Flöte und das Flötenspiel," and for doing this he gave me the original manuscript in his own hand writing.

Sincerely,

JAMES S. WILKINS, II."

An interesting correspondence developed, and extracts from later letters are as follows:

"I appreciate your efforts in doing reverence to Boehm, to the extent that, at the first safe opportunity I shall send you the original manuscript of "Die Flöte und das Flötenspiel," as a token, in Boehm's name, of my appreciation of the labor you have devoted to his work, and for your excellent translation. I know it would have pleased Mr. Boehm for you to receive it. * * *. I also send you as a part of your collection, a box-wood "Alt-flöte" tube, without keys, made in Mendler's shop; this was given to me by Boehm; it is a sample of a thinned-wood tube with raised finger holes. * * * I am sending a letter Boehm wrote me during a visit to Paris, as well as some leaves from my diary that may interest you—one has Mr. Boehm's autograph with an inscription. * * * I am also sending a biographical article which I wrote in Philadelphia in 1900.

With highest esteem, I am sincerely,

JAMES S. WILKINS, II."

Thus the translator came into possession of these most interesting mementos of Boehm, in May,

1909, shortly before the death of Mr. Wilkins. The necessity for a second edition of "The Flute and Flute-Playing," makes it possible to take advantage of this new material.

Boehm's manuscript in German is complete, and has been compared, paragraph by paragraph, with the printed edition; the differences are very few and are of no importance. Boehm's hand writing and his manuscript music are exceedingly neat and legible, as is shown by the reproductions of several pages in this book.

The text here given is a faithful, and usually a very literal, translation of the German. For the second edition the translation has been thoroughly revised so that it reads more smoothly, several hundred minor alterations having been made. Since Boehm's writings possess both a historical and a scientific interest, and his inventions have been the subject of much controversy, it has seemed desirable, in giving his descriptions and explanations, to retain as far as possible, the forms of expression and even the wording of the original. Some traces of the German constructions, no doubt remain. While a freer translation might be preferred by some, it is believed the one given is always intelligible and explicit. There has been a slight rearrangement of subject matter and of paragraphing. The use of emphasis—indicated by *italics* in English—which is very frequent in the original, has been omitted.

Eight errors in the original lithographed Tables of Fingerings, and a few typographical errors in the tables of acoustical numbers have been corrected; no other corrections have been found necessary.

All of the original illustrations, twelve line drawings and several note diagrams, are reproduced with only such alterations as are noted in the descriptive matter; the musical illustrations in Part II have been copied photographically from the German edition. The first English edition contained, in addition, one drawing, several note-diagrams, pictures of six flutes, and three portraits. This edition contains fifty-six illustrations, including the twelve original drawings, pictures of twenty-two flutes, views of Boehm's home, six portraits and facsimiles of manuscripts. There are also several additional drawings and note-diagrams in the text. Two of the three portraits which appeared in the previous edition have been reëngraved from newly found originals. The sources of the portraits are given in the List of Illustrations. All of the pictures of flutes (excepting the two drawings from Boehm's pamphlet of 1847) are photographic reproductions from instruments in the translator's historical collection.

For this edition the Introduction has been rewritten, and four appendices have been added; the latter contain biographical notes, a revised list of Boehm's musical compositions, a price-list of flutes as made by Boehm, and a short list of current books relating to the flute.

In order that the full effect of Boehm's contributions during his life-time, and also that the rela-

tions of these to the flute as it is today, may be
made evident, many annotations and illustrations
have been added to the original text; all such added
matter is enclosed in square brackets, [ ].
Twenty-five or more important annotations and
additions, besides numerous smaller ones, appear
for the first time in this edition. The annotations
have been confined, for the most part, to matters
of fact; while exception has been taken to some
of the opinions expressed by Boehm, this is not
the place for discussion which might lead to controversy. The additions relate largely to details
of dimensions and constructions of the flutes as
made by Boehm & Mendler when these instruments had attained their greatest perfection, in
the years from 1870 to 1880. Nothwithstanding it
is forty years since the death of Boehm, yet there
is published now for the first time, all the essential
dimensions of the flute as Boehm himself made it.
The dimensions are given both for the flute in C
and the flute in G.

While the preparation of this book has involved
much labor, it has been a genuine labor of love;
the volume has become almost a memorial to the
Flute of Boehm. It is hoped that the book will
make still better known Boehm's very careful and
complete investigations, and that it will lead to a
deeper appreciation of the debt of gratitude which
all flutists owe him for the remarkable mechanical
and artistic developments which have resulted
from his efforts.

The writer wishes to express his thanks to Theobald Boehm and his sisters, of Munich, grandchil-

dren of the inventor of the flute; when the writer first visited them, some years ago, they gave approval of this English edition, and they have very kindly expressed this sentiment in a letter, a portion of which precedes this preface. These friends have also given other assistance which is highly appreciated. He also wishes to thank his many friends who have very enthusiastically assisted in the collection of historical material, instruments, and illustrations, and whose interest in the flute has been a source of great inspiration and encouragement.

DAYTON C. MILLER.

Case School of Applied Science,
Cleveland, Ohio, June, 1922.

CONTENTS

PART II—FLUTE-PLAYING

APPENDIX

LIST OF ILLUSTRATIONS

PORTRAITS

FIGURES

TRANSLATOR'S INTRODUCTION

THEOBALD BOEHM, of Munich—born on April 9, 1794, died on November 25, 1881—a celebrated Royal Bavarian Court-Musician, and inventor of the modern flute, described his inventions in a treatise "Die Flöte und das Flötenspiel," which was published in pamphlet form, in Munich, in 1871. In the introduction to this work Boehm says: "My treatise, 'Ueber den Flötenbau und die neuesten Verbesserungen desselben,' (1847), seems to have had but little influence. There is need, therefore, of this work in which is given as complete a description as is possible of my flutes and instructions for handling them, and which also contains instructions upon the art of playing the flute with a pure tone and a good style."

In a letter to Mr. Broadwood, dated November 15, 1868, Boehm wrote: "I have at length finished it (this treatise) and will see about a publisher. There ought properly to be both a French and an English translation, but I cannot myself undertake them * * * . My treatise will contain chapters as follows: * * * ; and the history of all my work and all my experience during a period of sixty years will be contained in one little book."

"Die Flöte und das Flötenspiel," was read with great interest by the writer, and while upon a holiday some years ago, it was translated; others having expressed a desire to read the work in English, its publication was undertaken, the first English edition appearing in November, 1908.

While much has been written about the Boehm flute, Boehm's own publications seem not to have received the attention they deserve. Boehm submitted his new system flute of 1832 to the Paris Academy of Sciences, where its proper recognition was effectively prevented by the professional jealousy of Coche, who at the same time pretended to be giving friendly assistance. In 1847 Boehm published a small book of 59 pages entitled "Ueber den Flötenbau und die neuesten Verbesserungen desselben." A French translation of this work was published in 1848. Boehm himself prepared an English version which was published in London in 1882, under the title "An Essay on the Construction of Flutes," edited by W. S. Broadwood. Boehm exhibited his new flute with cylindrical bore at the London Exhibitions of 1851 and 1862, and at the Paris Expositions of 1855 and 1867. With the exhibits of 1862 and 1867 he submitted his *Schema* for locating the tone-holes according to a scientific method, the first ever applied to such an instrument. The judges, not appreciating the significance of the *Schema*, refused to recognize it as a meritorious contribution, thus again depriving Boehm of his just rewards. The *Schema* having been discredited by the judges, Boehm's only publication of it was a quite ineffective one in the journal of a local engineering society of Munich, in 1868. In 1871 Boehm published a second work in pamphlet form, "Die Flöte

und das Flötenspiel," the work herewith presented
in translation. After Boehm's death, one of the
judges of the 1867 Exposition, re-examined the
Schema and published, in 1882, his belated conclusion that its method is entirely correct and that
it was actually the basis of Boehm's own constructions.

Several years after Boehm had made known his
flute of 1832 with the new system of fingering, he
was accused, particularly by Coche of Paris, of
having taken important features of his system
from the work of an enthusiastic amateur experi-
menter by the name of Gordon. In answer to this
accusation Boehm wrote in his work of 1847 as
follows: "The surest proof of the authenticity of
my invention, I believe will be given by describ-
ing the motives which led me to its development,
and by explaining the acoustical and mechanical
principles of which I made application; for he
alone is capable of carrying out a rational work,
who is able to give a complete account of the why
and wherefore of every detail from its conception
to its completion." Judged by this criterion, Boehm
deserves the highest credit, for he has given an
account almost beyond criticism, and perhaps the
best ever given for any musical instrument, of
the why and wherefore of the flute.

After Boehm's death, the charge of misappro-
priating Gordon's invention was renewed in a bitter attack by Rockstro in his "Treatise on the
Flute." A very complete account of this controversy and of the historical events mentioned

above, together with a critical analysis of all the evidence, is given in Welch's "History of the Boehm Flute." Welch's investigations completely exonerate Boehm of any improper use of Gordon's work, and fully establish his title to the system which bears his name.

In the pamphlet of 1847 stress was put upon the so-called scientific construction of the flute; in the present treatise the treatment is more complete and practical and the scientific portions appear in truer relations to the subject. To one who reads understandingly it is evident that, while the general treatment of the principles of the flute is a scientific one, the actual dimensions for construction are based upon experiment. Having determined by experiment, the fundamental length of the octave with a flute tube of given dimensions, the locations of all the holes for a flute of any desired pitch are found by the application of simple laws of acoustics. Although no complete set of laws has yet been formulated which enable one to calculate all the dimensions of a flute, this fact in no way lessens the value of Boehm's work. While his greatest desire was to elevate the art of music, he was possessed of the true scientific spirit; his purposes were conceived and carried out according to scientific methods; his finished work was the best practical realization of his ideals and he has described his designs and practical constructions very explicitly. The flute which he revolutionized and developed within a period of fifty years, has not been essentially improved during the subsequent fifty years.

The full consideration of Boehm's contributions must be left for a later work; but to him we certainly owe the present system of fingering—an astonishingly perfect one—the cylinder bore, the silver tube and much of the beautiful mechanism which have completely revolutionized the instrument and have made the Boehm flute one of the most perfect of musical instruments. When one remembers that the flute has been known since prehistoric time, and that its form in the year 1800 is fairly represented by the picture of Boehm's first flute, then a mere glance at the illustration of Boehm's perfected silver flute of 1878, makes it seem almost impossible that such a development could have taken place within the life-time of one man, much less that it could have resulted largely from the investigations and efforts of one man. The musical effects of the flute as perceived by the ear have been improved quite as much as have the mechanical features as seen by the eye. The flute has thus become not only more useful to the professional musician, but it has become an exceedingly attractive and delightful instrument for the amateur. The Boehm flute is, *par excellence,* the instrument for the enthusiastic lover of chamber music.

The flute has always been a favorite instrument with gentlemen performers; it is today, more than ever before, the gentleman's instrument. But the flute of Boehm, made of silver, has an artistic symmetry and beauty, combined with lightness, which renders it as attractive in appearance as it is rich in tone. The sound is produced with the slightest effort; one has only to breathe into the embouchure. The natural position in holding the instrument is characterized by an easy gracefulness; its manipulation in general requires delicacy of manner. Boehm's improvements have greatly enhanced these qualities, and now the flute is preeminently suited for use as a lady's instrument.

One of Boehm's real contributions which the musical world has been slow to appreciate, is the flute in G, the Bass Flute. Boehm made this instrument entirely practicable for musical purposes, and it has tonal qualities that should have given it prominence long ago. It is hoped that not only flutists, but composers, directors, and auditors, will very soon realize the beauties of this instrument, and that its use will be greatly stimulated.

While this work is devoted to the flute, yet flutists will the better realize the value of Boehm's contributions, by keeping in mind the fact that they were of wide application. His researches in connection with the flute and its theory played an important part in the development of other instruments, such as the clarinet, oboe, and bassoon. No history of these instruments can be complete without including references to Boehm's work. He contributed to a very important phase of the development of the modern piano, the method of "overstringing." Boehm spent several years in investigations quite foreign to the world of music, in the development of improved methods for the purification of iron and for the manufacture of steel directly from iron; his contributions were certainly of fundamental importance. He also invented a new device for transmitting rotatory motion, which, if not important, is interesting and was deemed worthy of a silver medal. Several of these diverse interests are referred to in the Appendix.

Boehm was an extraordinary artist, and he was possessed of the true scientific spirit of research; he was a man of great versatility and of profound mental ability: he is more than worthy of all the honor that he has received.

PART I

—

THE FLUTE

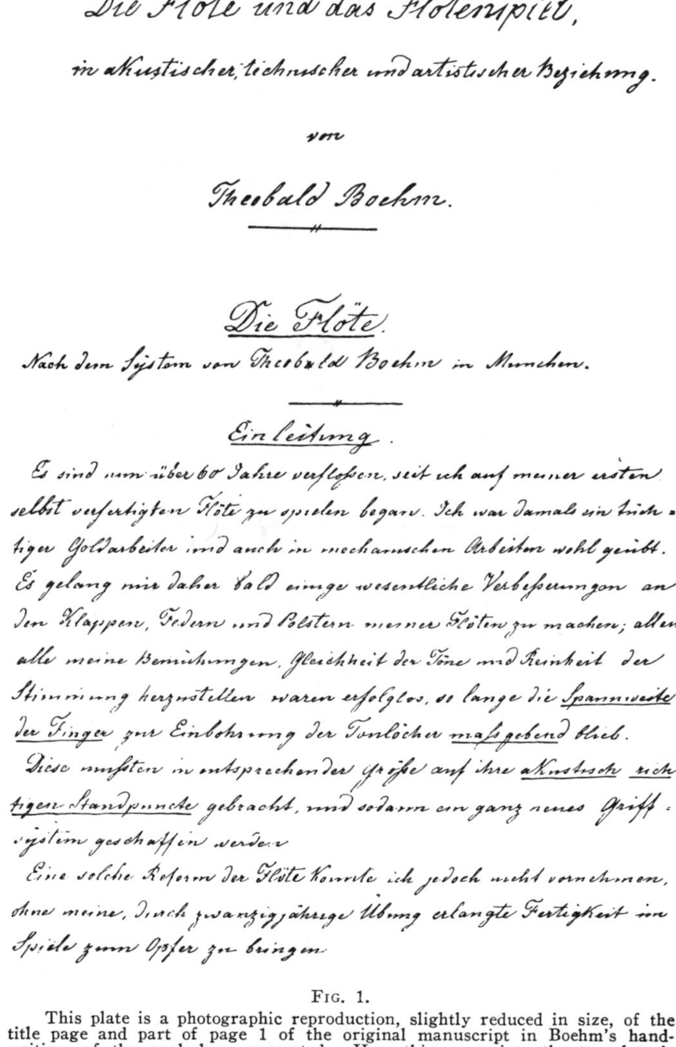

Die Flöte und das Flötenspiel,

in akustischer, technischer und artistischer Beziehung.

von

Theobald Boehm.

Die Flöte.

Nach dem System von Theobald Boehm in München.

Einleitung.

Es sind nun über 60 Jahre verflossen, seit ich auf meiner ersten selbst verfertigten Flöte zu spielen begann. Ich war damals ein tüchtiger Goldarbeiter und auch in mechanischen Arbeiten wohl geübt. Es gelang mir daher bald einige wesentliche Verbesserungen an den Klappen, Federn und Polstern meiner Flöten zu machen; allein alle meine Bemühungen, Gleichheit der Töne und Reinheit der Stimmung herzustellen, waren erfolglos, so lange die Spannweite der Finger zur Einbohrung der Tonlöcher maßgebend blieb.

Diese mußten in entsprechender Größe auf ihre akustisch richtigere Standpuncte gebracht, und sodann ein ganz neues Griffsystem geschaffen werden.

Eine solche Reform der Flöte konnte ich jedoch nicht vornehmen, ohne meine, durch zwanzigjährige Übung erlangte Fertigkeit im Spiele zum Opfer zu bringen.

FIG. 1.

This plate is a photographic reproduction, slightly reduced in size, of the title page and part of page 1 of the original manuscript in Boehm's handwriting, of the work here presented. How this came into the translator's possession is told in the preface.

THE FLUTE
AND FLUTE-PLAYING

PART I—THE FLUTE
UPON THE SYSTEM OF
THEOBALD BOEHM
OF MUNICH

I.   INTRODUCTION

IT is now more than sixty years since I began
to play upon the first flute of my own construction.   I was at that time a proficient goldsmith
and was also skilled in the mechanic arts.   I soon
endeavored to make essential improvements in the
keys, springs, and pads of my flute; but, notwithstanding all my efforts, equality of tone and perfection of tuning were impossible, because the
proper spacing of the tone-holes required too great
a spreading of the fingers.   In order that the tone-
holes might be made of proper size and be placed
at the acoustically correct points, it was necessary
to devise an entirely new system of fingering.   The
application of this system required a remodeling
of the flute which I was unable to accomplish
without sacrificing my facility in playing which
had been acquired by twenty years of practice.

["As a child Boehm was charmed by music, and
he learned by himself to play the flageolet; when

FIG. 2.
Boehm's first flute, played by him when
he was about fifteen years old

this no longer satisfied him, he took up the flute."
Fig. 2 is a picture of what was probably Boehm's
first flute, here referred to. This instrument has
recently been obtained from Mr. Franz Rath of
San Diego, California, and is now in the translator's historical collection of flutes. Mr. Rath
supplies the following information. Boehm owned
this flute in his boyhood; as his proficiency developed he needed a flute with more keys, and
about 1810, when he was sixteen years old, he
sold this one to his chum, Ferinand Marker. Herr
Marker removed to Vienna about 1820, and later
taught his grandson, Franz Rath, to play the flute
and gave him the old flute of Boehm's about 1874.
Mr. Rath came to America in 1887 bringing the
flute with him, and it has remained in his possession till the present time, 1920. The flute is of
boxwood, stained and cracked, as might be expected after having served several young flute
players. The maker's name, PROSER, is stamped on
each joint. "At the age of sixteen years (in 1810)
he made for himself an instrument patterned after
one with four keys, (from the workshop of the
celebrated Karl August Grenser of Dresden),
which had been loaned him by a friend. Then
he began to blow the flute with gleeful enthusiasm
in all his spare time, not especially to the delight
of his friends and neighbors. Among them was
Johann Nepomuk Capeller, at that time flutist in
the Court Orchestra, who, one day, happened to
meet the budding virtuoso on the stairway and
he laughingly said: 'You, young flute-player, I cannot endure your noisy blowing any longer; come

to me and I will show you how it ought to be done.'
Naturally it was not necessary to say this twice to
young Boehm. He became Capeller's most zealous
pupil and, notwithstanding he had but little time
to devote to the flute, his passionate fondness for
the instrument caused such rapid progress that,
after scarcely two years of practice, he created
astonishment by public performances." — The
quoted sentences have been translated from the
privately-printed booklet, *Zur Erinnerung an
Theobald Boehm,* presented by Boehm's grandchildren.   Much the same account is given in
Schafhautl's "Life of Boehm," which is a part
of Welch's "History of the Boehm Flute."]

[“With my progress in flute-playing there developed, naturally, a desire for better instruments.
In 1812 I was already the first flutist in the Royal
Isarthor Theater in Munich. In the years between
this and 1817, by using the facilities of my goldsmith's shop which had the usual equipment and
which was further supplied with the necessary
machinery, I made many flutes, for myself and
others, according to the best models of the time
and also with many original improvements * *
such as new types of springs, linings and corks
for the joints, a moveable gold embouchure, and
others. After I obtained my appointment to the
Royal Court Chapel in 1818 the business of goldsmith was given up and I devoted myself entirely
to music. For some years, because of the lack of
my own shop, I had flutes made according to my
designs by other makers; however, the instruments
thus obtained were not satisfactory, and, finally,

in order to carry out my own ideas without hindrance, I decided to establish my own flute factory. In October, 1828, I was again at work in my well-equipped shop, and began to construct various machines and appliances for making with more facility and accuracy a better key mechanism than had previously been in use. Among these devices was one for screwing the metal posts into the wood accurately in the line of radius of the bore; another was for boring the holes in the spherical heads of the pillars. These and numerous other devices secured the easy and certain operation of all parts of the mechanism. By the end of the year the first flute was finished, having a new key mechanism which was both solid and elegant in construction, and the flute met with general approbation as to quality of tone and intonation, and was widely adopted. In the year 1831 I played in Paris and London upon such a flute of the ordinary system which had been made in my workshop in Munich."—From Boehm's pamphlet of 1847, *Ueber den Flötenbau und die neuesten Verbesserungen desselben.* Fig. 3 is the drawing of this flute which accompanies the above description, and to which Boehm has attached the date 1829. In February, 1922, the translator received from Mr. Arthur Gemeinhardt of Markneukirchen, a rare specimen of this identical type, made in Boehm's shop, which is shown in Fig. 5. This flute is of cocus-wood, with silver keys and flat gold springs, with workmanship and finish which are perfect; it is certainly superior to any other contemporary flute which has been examined, and comparable with the later instruments of Boehm & Mendler. The tone is very beautiful, sweet and mellow, and, of course, not powerful; the tuning is astonishingly good considering that it is a flute of the old system.   The flute bears the inscription BOEHM & GREVE A MUNICH.   Grevé was Boehm's chief workman and partner, and is known to have been with him at least from 1830 to 1843.]

Notwithstanding all my success as an artist, the defects of my instrument remained perceptible, and finally I decided, in 1832, to construct my ring-keyed flute, upon which I played in London and Paris in the following year, where its advantages were at once recognized by the greatest artists and by *l'Académie des sciences.*

[In a letter to Mr. Broadwood, dated August, 1871, Boehm writes: "I did as well as any continental flutist could have done, in London, in 1831, but I could not match Nicholson in power of tone, wherefore I set to work to remodel my flute.   Had I not heard him, probably the Boehm flute would never have been made."]

As compared with the old flute, this one was unquestionably much nearer perfection.   The tone-holes were placed in their acoustically correct position and, through my new system of fingering, one could play all possible tone combinations clearly and surely.   As regards the sounding and the quality of the lower and the higher tones, there was yet much to be desired, but further improvements could be secured only by a complete change in the bore of the flute tube.

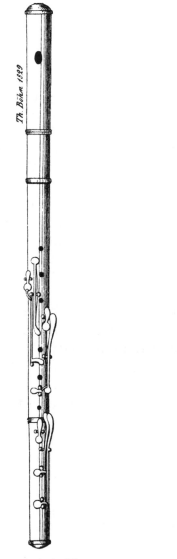

FIG. 3. Boehm's Flute
Old System. 1829.

FIG. 4. Boehm's Flute
New System. 1832.

[The drawing, Fig. 4, is reproduced from Boehm's pamphlet of 1847, and shows the first Boehm-System Flute, originated in 1832, with ring-keys and conical bore. Boehm made arrangements to have his new-system flute manufactured in London by Rudall and Rose and in Paris by Godfroy. Fig. 6 shows an excellent specimen of this type made by Godfroy about 1840. It differs from Boehm's own model only in that it has the Dorus G♯ key (see page 64) instead of the open G♯ key.]

The method of boring, with a cylindrical head and a conical contraction in the lower part, which was first applied by Christopher Denner of Nuremberg (born in 1655, died in 1707), and later was improved by Quantz [1697-1773], Tromlitz [1726-1805], and others, was nevertheless far from being in accordance with acoustical principles, as the positions of the finger-holes had been borrowed from the primitive *Schwegel* or *Querpfeife*. This conical bore was in use for more than a century and a half, during which time no one was able to devise a better form.

I was never able to understand why, of all wind instruments with tone-holes and conical bore, the flute alone should be blown at its wider end; it seems much more natural that, with a rising pitch and shorter length of air column, the diameter should become smaller. I experimented with tubes of various bores but I soon found that, with only empirical experiments, a satisfactory result would be difficult of attainment.

[The flute of 1832 with conical bore and ring

FIG. 5.
Old-System Flute
by Boehm & Grevé
Model of 1829

FIG. 6.
Boehm-System Flute
by Godfroy
Model of 1840

FIG. 7.
Cylinder Flute No. 19
by Th. Boehm
Model of 1850

keys, therefore, remained unchanged for fifteen years. Boehm says in his treatise of 1847: "With regard to all the other alterations or improvements which have since been made in the flute (between the years 1832 and 1846), whose value or worthlessness I leave for others to decide, I had no part in them. From the year 1833 to the year 1846 I was unable to devote my time to the manufacture of instruments, being otherwise engaged [in iron and steel work] and for this reason my flute factory was·given up eight years ago, in 1839."]

I finally called science to my aid and gave two years [1846-1847] to the study of the principles of acoustics under the excellent guidance of Herr Professor Dr. Carl von Schafhäutl [of the University of Munich. An account of Schafhäutl's life and work by Herr Ludwig Boehm appeared in the *Bayer Industrie und Gewerbeblatt,* No. 17, 1890. A translation of this memoir is given in Welch's "History of the Boehm Flute," pages 348-372]. After making many experiments, as precise as possible, I finished a flute in the later part of 1847, founded upon scientific principles, for which I received the highest prize at the World's Expositions, in London in 1851, and in Paris in 1855.

[Fig. 7 is a picture of the metal flute with cylindrical bore and covered keys invented in 1847. This instrument, made by Boehm himself, is No. 19 of the series beginning in 1847. It belonged to Edward Martin Heindl, one of Boehm's most famous pupils, who lived with Boehm for four years from 1847 to 1851. Heindl came to America in

1864, bringing this flute, which is probably the first cylinder-bore, metal Boehm flute used in this country. Heindl played this instrument for many years while he was a member of the Mendelssohn Quintette Club of Boston, and after he became first flutist of the Boston Symphony Orchestra, upon its organization in 1881. See pages 28, 95 and 99.]

Since this time my flutes have come to be played in all the countries of the world, yet my treatise, *Ueber den Flötenbau und die neuesten Verbesserungen desselben,* published before that time [in 1847] by B. Schott's Söhne of Mainz, which contains complete explanations of my system with the dimensions and numerical proportions, seems to have had but little influence. Because of the many questions which are continually being asked of me concerning the advantages and management of my flute, it is evident that the acoustical proportions and key mechanism are not sufficiently well understood to enable one to help himself in case of accidental troubles and derangements.

There is need, therefore, of this work, which will be welcomed by all flute players, in which is given as complete a description as is possible of my flutes, and instructions for handling them, and which also contains instructions upon the art of playing the flute with a pure tone and a good style.

II. THE ACOUSTICAL PROPORTIONS OF THE FLUTE

[The original manuscript of this work contains a page which has been crossed out by a pencil mark, and which does not appear in the first printed edition. While this portion, consisting of the first three following paragraphs, is not important, nevertheless it forms an appropriate introduction to this chapter.]

ALL of my flutes consist of three pieces, the head-joint, the middle-joint, and the foot. When these pieces are joined together they form the tube of the flute, which is closed above the mouthhole by a cork plug. The main part of the tube is cylindrical, with an inside diameter of 19 millimeters. The bore of the head-joint is gradually reduced in diameter by two millimeters, from the joint upwards to the cork. The free speech of the tone and the correct tuning of the higher octaves depend upon the particular form of this curvilinear reduction in the diameter.

The air column enclosed by the tube of the flute is set into vibration by blowing across the mouthhole, causing the fundamental tone to sound. The pitch of this tone depends upon the total length of the vibrating column of air measured from the cork to the lower end of the tube. The higher tones of the first octave are obtained by shortening the length of the vibrating column of air, for which purpose lateral tone-holes are bored in the tube. The holes should be as large as is possible, since the effective shortening of the tube is proportional to the ratio of the size of the hole to the diameter of the bore.

The correct intonation of a tone depends, consequently, not only upon the distance of the hole from the upper end of the air column, but also upon its size, and therefore the exact place where the hole is located must be determined by accurate computation. All the formulae for these calculations, as well as other theoretical explanations have previously been given in my treatise *Ueber den Flötenbau,* already mentioned.

[The metric system is used throughout in giving the dimensions of the flute. For conversion, the following equivalents may be used: 1 inch=25.40 millimeters; 1 millimeter=0.03937 inch; 1 ounce avoirdupois=28.35 grams; 1 ounce Troy=31.10 grams].

All wind instruments with tone- or finger-holes, whose construction requires very accurate proportions, can be improved only through the investigation of the principles of both the good and the bad of existing instruments, and through a rational application of the results; the greatest possible perfection will be obtained only when theory and practice go hand in hand. When the calculation of the required data is undertaken, the questions first to be investigated are the dimensions and numerical proportions of the air columns and tone-holes of each separate instrument.

For this purpose I had prepared, in 1846, a great number of conical and cylindrical tubes of various dimensions, and of many metals and several kinds of wood, so that the relative fitness of each as to pitch, ease of sounding and quality of tone, could be fundamentally investigated.

The most desirable proportions of the air column, that is, the dimensions of bore best suited for bringing out the fundamental tones at various pitches, were soon found. These experiments show:

1. That the strength, as well as the full, clear quality of the fundamental tone, is proportional to the volume of the air set in vibration.

2. That a more or less important contraction in the bore of the upper part of the flute tube, and a shortening or lengthening of this contraction, have an important influence upon the production of the tones and upon the tuning of the octaves.

3. That this contraction must be made in a certain geometrical proportion, which is closely approached by the curve of the parabola.

4. That the formation of the nodes and segments of the sound waves takes place most easily and perfectly in a cylindrical flute tube, the length of which is thirty times its diameter, and in which the contraction begins in the upper fourth part of the length of the tube, continuing to the cork where the diameter is reduced one tenth part.

[Perhaps flutists are more puzzled by the "parabolic head-joint" than by any other feature of the modern flute. The contraction in the bore is undoubtedly determined by experiment, and not by any mathematical calculation based upon the properties of the parabola. The translator has measured and plotted the curves of perhaps a hundred flutes, among which are specimens of nearly every celebrated make. Most of these curves do not in any way resemble a parabola; such resemblance as is possessed by the few may be described by saying that the curve which at first departs but little from the straight line, bends more and more rapidly as it progresses. But sometimes the portion with the greatest curvature is next to the cork and sometimes next to the tuning slide!]

[The "parabolic" contraction in the head-joint of an excellent specimen of Boehm & Mendler flute is shown in Fig. 8. At the right is the section of the tube, drawn in full size. The length of the tapered portion is 134 millimeters. Starting at the cork, where the diameter of the bore is 17.1 millimeters, the horizontal dotted lines indicate the sections increasing in diameter, successively, by 0.1 millimeter, up to 19.0 millimeters, near the tuning slide. The figures on the dotted lines are the diameters of the tube at the various sections. At the left is an exaggerated diagram of the actual contraction in this specimen of flute; the horizontal scale for this part of the figure is 50 times the vertical scale. If the bore of the tube were

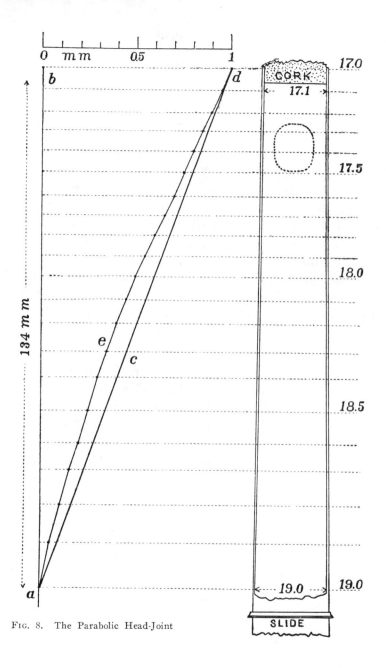

Fig. 8. The Parabolic Head-Joint

cylindrical, one side of it would be represented by the line *ab;* if it contracted by a straight taper, the line *acd* would represent the inner surface of the tube; the "parabolic" curve actually existing is shown by the curved line *aed*.]

Since the dimensions most suitable for the formation of the fundamental tones correspond closely to those of theory, a flute of these dimensions, the length of the air column being 606 millimeters and the diameter 20 millimeters, [because of the larger diameter, the length of tube required is somewhat less than that given on page 35 for a tube 19 millimeters in diameter] would certainly be perfect as regards a pure, full tone and ease of sounding through a compass of about two octaves. But in order to extend the compass to three full octaves as now required [in flute music] I decided for the sake of freedom in the upper tones, to reduce the diameter to 19 millimeters, notwithstanding that this injured to some extent the beauty of the tones of the first two octaves.

[In a letter written in 1867 Boehm says: "I have made several flutes with a bore 20 millimeters in diameter, therefore one millimeter wider than usual; the first and second octaves were better, but of course the third octave was not so good. I could, indeed still play up to C_6, but from $F_5\sharp$ upwards the notes were sounded with difficulty, and if my lip did not happen to be in good order, I could not sound the higher notes *piano* at all. The flute, whether in the orchestra or in solo playing, is treated as the next highest instrument after the piccolo; modern composers do not hesitate to write for it up to C_6; therefore the bore of 19 millimeters diameter is certainly the best for general purposes."]

[The silver flute with a wood head-joint which is shown in Fig. 32 has a bore of 20 millimeters; it is the only flute in C of this bore which the translator has seen. Its tone quality has been directly compared with that of other Boehm & Mendler flutes having a bore of 19 millimeters. The result of the comparison was to corroborate the opinions of Boehm as expressed above.]

[Before the year 1865 Boehm had developed the "Alt-Flöte," commonly called the "Bass Flute," which is described in Chapter XII; the tube of this instrument has an inside diameter of 26 millimeters. Messrs. Rudall, Carte and Company have long made such bass flutes and also the "Alto Flute" in Bb, having a bore of 20.5 millimeters. These instruments are altogether practicable and have the beautiful tone quality in the lower octaves, referred to above.]

A second obstacle which compelled me to depart from the theory was the impossibility of making a movable cork or stopper in the upper end of the flute, so that its distance from the center of the embouchure might be decreased or increased in proportion to the pitch of each tone; a medium position for it must therefore be chosen which will best serve for both the highest and the lowest tones; this position was found to be 17 millimeters from the center of the embouchure.

Next, the size and form of the mouth-hole (embouchure) must be determined. The tone-producing current of air must be blown against the sharp edge of the mouth-hole, at an angle which varies with the pitch of the tone. When the air stream strikes the edge of the hole it is broken, or rather divided, so that one part of it goes over or beyond the hole, while the greater part, especially with a good embouchure, produces tone and acts upon the column of air enclosed by the tube, setting it into vibration.

By this means the molecular vibrations [see page 53] of the tube are excited, producing a tone as long as the air stream is maintained; it follows therefore that the tone will be stronger the greater the number of the air particles acting upon the tone-producing air column in a given time. The opening between the lips through which the stream of air passes is in the form of a slit, and a mouth-hole in shape like an elongated rectangle with rounded corners, presenting a long edge to the wide air stream, will allow more air to be effective than would a round or oval hole of equal size.

[Figs. 9 and 10 are photographs of the embouchures of two excellent flutes, shown somewhat larger than full size, representing the oval and rounded-square shapes. The latter is a perfect specimen of the Boehm & Mendler type. The selection of shape and size of embouchure seems to be largely one of individual choice or habit; an embouchure which one performer finds to be excellent another cannot use.]

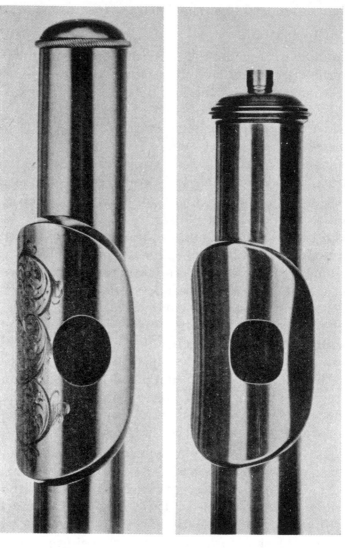

FIG. 9.
Elliptical Embouchure
Rudall, Carte & Co.

FIG. 10.
Rectangular Embouchure
Boehm & Mendler

For the same reason a larger mouth-hole will produce a louder tone than a smaller one, but this requires a greater strength in the muscles of the lip, because there is formed a hollow space under the lip which is unsupported. More than this, it is often difficult to keep the air current directed at the proper angle, upon which the intonation and the tone quality for the most part depend.

By a greater depression of the air stream towards the middle of the hole, the tone becomes deeper and more pungent, while a greater elevation makes the tone higher and more hollow. Consequently the angle between the sides of the mouth-hole and the longitudinal section through the axis of the air column, as well as the height of these sides, has an important influence upon the easy production of the tone. In my opinion an angle of 7 degrees is best adapted to the entire compass of tones, the walls being 4.2 millimeters

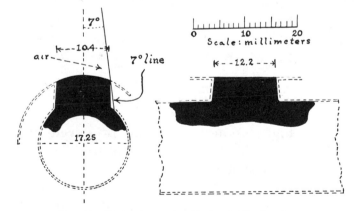

FIG. 11. Embouchure of a Boehm & Mendler flute.
Transverse and longitudinal sections.

thick; and a mouth-hole 10 millimeters wide and 12 millimeters long, is best suited to most flute players.

[The measurements of many Boehm & Mendler flutes show sizes slightly larger than that mentioned, the average being 10.4 millimeters by 12.2 millimeters (0.409 inch by 0.480 inch).]

[The shape of a blow-hole may be clearly seen from a wax impression; Fig. 11 shows transverse and longitudinal sections of a gold embouchure on a Boehm & Mendler flute. The cut is made photographically from the actual wax casts, and is slightly larger than full size. This blow-hole has sides which are straight and nearly parallel. The 7° of undercutting mentioned by Boehm, indicated by the solid line in the figure, is not present. Some of the earlier flutes by Boehm show a slight undercutting, but the later ones, both of wood and silver, have the sides nearly parallel, as shown in this instance.]

Upon the completion of these experiments I constructed many thin, hard-drawn tubes of brass upon which the fundamental tone C_3,

and also higher notes, could be produced by a breath and be brought to any desired strength without their rising in pitch.

The fact that the hissing noise heard in other flutes was not perceptible convinced me that the correct dimensions of the tube, and its smooth inner surface permitted the formation of the sound waves without noticeable friction. From this as well as from the fine quality of tone of the harmonics or acoustical over-tones, can be inferred the perfect fitness of my tube for the flute; and with this I began the determination of the amount of shortening or cutting of the air column, required for producing the intervals of the first octave.

The simplest and shortest method is, naturally, successively to cut off from the lower end of the flute tube so much as will make the length of the air column correspond to each tone of the chromatic scale. In order that these proportions might be accurately verified, I made a tube in which all the twelve tone sections could be taken off and again put together, and which was provided with a sliding joint in the upper part of the tube to correct for any defects in tuning.

Since a flute cannot be made to consist of many separate pieces, all the tone lengths must be combined in one tube and these lengths must be determined by laterally bored holes; the air column may be considered as disconnected or cut off by these holes in a degree determined by the ratio between the diameters of the holes and of the tube.

The effective air column, however, is not as much shortened by a tone-hole as it would be by cutting the tube at the same point. Even if the size of the hole is equal to the diameter of the tube, yet the air waves will not pass out of the hole at a right angle as freely as along the axis.

The waves meet with a resistance from the air contained in the lower part of the tube, which is so considerable that all the tones are much too flat when they come from holes placed at the points determined by actually cutting the tube. And, moreover, the height of the sides of the holes adds to the flattening effect. The tone-holes must, therefore, be placed nearer the mouth-hole the smaller their diameter and the higher their sides.

Although one octave can be correctly tuned in this manner using small holes, yet for the following reasons it is greatly to be desired that the tone-holes should be as large as possible.

1. Free and therefore powerful tones can be obtained only from large holes which are placed as nearly as possible in their acoustically correct positions.

2. If the holes are small and are considerably removed from their proper places, the formation of the nodes of vibration is disturbed and rendered uncertain; the tone is produced with difficulty, and often breaks into other tones corresponding to the other aliquot parts of the air column [harmonics].

3. The smaller the holes, the more distorted become the tone waves, rendering the tone dull and of poor quality.

4. The pure intonation of the third octave depends particularly upon the correct position of the holes.

From accurate investigations it is shown that the disadvantages just mentioned, become imperceptible only when the size of the holes is, at the least, three-fourths of the diameter of the tube [14¼ millimeters]. But in the manufacture of wooden flutes, the making of holes of such a size causes considerable difficulty. At first it appeared very desirable to make the holes of gradually increasing size from the upper to the lower ones; later this proved to be very disadvantageous and again I concluded that a medium course is the best. Therefore I finally chose a constant diameter for all the twelve tone-holes from C_3♯ to C_4, which for silver flutes is 13.5 millimeters, and for wooden flutes 13 millimeters.

[Actual measurements of many Boehm & Mendler flutes usually show tone-holes for both the body and foot-joints of wooden flutes which are uniformly 12.8 millimeters in diameter. A few flutes only have holes full 13 millimeters in diameter. The largest size of hole found on the body-joint of a silver flute is 13.4 millimeters, while the usual size is 13.2 millimeters for both body and foot-joint. The Macauley flute, Fig. 31, No. 12, and also Fig. 34, has holes on the body (nine holes) 13.2 millimeters in diameter, while the four holes on the B♮ foot-joint are 14.5 millimeters in diameter. This enlargement of the holes on the foot-joint is seldom found on Boehm's flutes, but it is common in flutes of modern manufacture. The Shippen flute, Fig. 31, No. 13, and also Fig. 32, with a bore 20 millimeters, has the five upper holes on the body (G♯, A, A♯, B, and C thumb-key) of a diameter of 14.0 millimeters while the four lower holes on the body and the four holes on the B♮ foot-joint have a uniform diameter of 15 millimeters.]

[The Heindl flute, illustrated in Fig. 7 and in the group picture, Fig. 31, was made about 1850, and has graduated tone-holes. The thumb-key hole for C_4 is 11.4 millimeters in diameter, and the low C♯ hole is 13.6 millimeters in diameter; the sizes of the holes increase uniformly, each being 0.2 millimeter larger in diameter than the preceding hole. A letter written by Boehm, in 1862, to Louis Lot, the celebrated flute-maker of Paris, says regarding graduated tone-holes: "The flute-playing world knows that for six years I made all my silver flutes with graduated holes. During my stay in London in 1851, I, myself, used a flute with graduated holes. The smallest, the thumb-key hole for C_4 was 12 millimeters in diameter, and the largest, that for C_3♯, 15 millimeters, a constant gradation of a quarter of a millimeter. The graduated holes are in my opinion the best, but the difference is scarcely appreciable. I have discontinued making them on account of the greater difficulty in the manufacture." The last sentence seems to state three facts regarding graduated holes; they are the best; their superiority is slight; the cost of manufacture is greater. Today nearly all makers use at least two sizes of holes, and some use three or more sizes, for the regular tone-holes.]

With these dimensions, in order to produce the correct pitch, the center of the C_3♯ hole must be moved 5 millimeters above the point at which the tube would have to be cut off in order to produce the same tone. The amount of removal increases with each hole in the ascending scale, so that the C_4 hole [thumb-key hole] must be placed 12 millimeters above the point of section of the air column. In this manner the correct positions of the holes are obtained, and the tuning of all the notes of the first octave is rendered, to the ear, as perfect as possible.

The notes of the second octave are produced, as it were, by overblowing the tones of the first, by narrowing the opening in the lips, and by changing the angle and increasing the speed of the stream of air; this results in the formation of shorter tone-waves.

In order to secure a greater compass of tones [in the higher octaves], it is necessary to use a narrower tube than is best suited to the lower tones, or, in other words, a tube which has a diameter too small in proportion to its length. From this it results that the tones D_4 and $D_4\sharp$

[being sounded as harmonics of a long, slender tube] are of different quality from the next following tones, and it is first with the tone E_4 that a suitable relation between the length and width of the tube is again restored.

The flute properly should have three additional large holes for the tones $C_4\sharp$, D_4, $D_4\sharp$.

Following the theory, the octave holes for D_4 and $D_4\sharp$ would also serve as vent holes for the twelfths, $G_5\sharp$ and A_5, giving all of these tones a better quality, a purer intonation, and a freer sounding. But there is only one finger available, and this must be used for $C_4\sharp$; and as I was unwilling to make my key system still more complicated, the $C_4\sharp$ hole must be so placed that it may serve at the same time as a so-called vent hole for the tones, D_4, $D_4\sharp$, D_5, $G_5\sharp$, and A_5.

[Thus the theoretical position of the $C_4\sharp$ hole was abandoned] and it was necessary to determine by experiment a size and position for the $C_4\sharp$ hole which would satisfy all of these demands. It was found that the $C_4\sharp$ hole, as well as the two small holes for the D_4 and $D_4\sharp$ trill-keys, must therefore be placed considerably above their true positions, and must be made correspondingly smaller. [The sizes and positions of these holes are given on page 35.]

For the exact determination of these positions and the other tuning proportions, I had a flute made with movable holes, and was thus enabled to adjust all the tones higher or lower at pleasure. In this way I could easily determine the best positions of the upper three small holes, but it was not possible to determine the tuning of the other tones as perfectly as I desired; for, in endeavoring to produce an entire true scale in one key, the tones were always thrown out of the proportions of the equal temperament, without which the best possible tuning of wind instruments with tone-holes cannot be obtained.

Therefore, in order to determine with perfect accuracy the points at which the tone-holes shall be bored, one must avail himself of the help of theory. To form a basis for all the calculations of dimensions, and for the easy understanding of this, it seems not out of place to give as simply as possible an explanation of the fundamental acoustical laws.

As is known, the acuteness or graveness of a tone depends upon the length and volume of the sounding body, being proportional to the velocity of vibration which can be impressed upon the body. For the entire compass of musical tones, these fixed relative proportions have long been known with mathematical precision; the following Table I gives these relations for all the tones of the equally tempered scale in the form of vibration numbers and string lengths. [The ratio of the number of vibrations of any tone in the equally tempered scale to the number of vibrations of the preceding tone is the twelfth root of 2; the numerical value of this ratio is 1.059463. As the numbers in this table are useful for various acoustical computations, they have been recomputed by the translator, and several typographical errors in Boehm's figures have been corrected.]

TABLE I

Tones	Relative Vibration Numbers	Relative String Lengths
C_{x+1}	2.000000	0.500000
B	1.887749	0.529732
B♭ or A♯	1.781797	0.561231
A	1.681793	0.594604
A♭ or G♯	1.587401	0.629960
G	1.498307	0.667420
G♭ or F♯	1.414214	0.707107
F	1.334840	0.749154
E	1.259921	0.793701
E♭ or D♯	1.189207	0.840896
D	1.122462	0.890899
D♭ or C♯	1.059463	0.943874
C_x	1.000000	1.000000

Here is shown the geometrical progression in which the vibration frequency of C_x, which is designated the fundamental, is constantly increased throughout the scale, so that the number of vibrations of the octave, C_{x+1} has become double that of C_x; at the same time, shortening in equal progression, the string length is reduced from 1.0 to 0.5.

With these relative numbers it is a simple matter to calculate the absolute vibration-numbers corresponding to any desired pitch, since any given vibration number bears to each of the other intervals exactly the same proportion, as the relative number corresponding to this tone bears to the relative numbers of these other intervals.

For example, to calculate the number of vibrations of the tone C_3, knowing the absolute number of vibrations of the Normal A_3 to be 435 vibrations per second we have the following proportion:

relative A_3 : relative C_3=absolute A_3 : absolute C_3

1.681793 : 1.000000=435 : x

$$\frac{435 \times 1.000000}{1.681793} = 258.65$$

If now this absolute number 258.65 be multiplied by each of the relative vibration numbers of the above table, one obtains the absolute vibration numbers of all the tones in one octave of the normal scale from C_3 to C_4 [see Table II, page 35]. In this way one avoids the division by numbers of many places, which is necessary in the direct method of calculation.

In a similar way one calculates measurements of length, as soon as the theoretical length of the air column in any given system, corresponding to the string length 1.000000, is determined.

While the vibration numbers and theoretical proportions of lengths for all instruments remain always the same, yet the actual lengths of the air columns are very different, because each wind instrument has its own peculiar length in consequence of its method of tone formation. For example, an oboe and likewise a clarinet (on account of the flattening effect upon the tone of the tube and mouth-piece) are much shorter than a flute of the same pitch; and even in the flute the actual length of the air column is less than the theoretical length corresponding to the given tone. The same is true to a less extent of a simple tube or a mouth-piece alone. Hence it happens that a wind instrument cut in two in its middle does not given the octave of its fundamental, but a considerably flatter tone.

In the case of the flute the flattening influence of the cork, the mouth-hole, the tone-holes, and the dimensions of bore is such that, altogether, it amounts to an air column of 51.5 millimeters in length, which in the calculation must be considered theoretically as existing, in order that the length of the air column shall exactly correspond to the length of the string of the monochord determined from the numbers and proportions of the table.

It will be found that the actual length of the air column (and therefore also of the flute tube) from the center of a C_3 hole, bored in the side of a long flute tube [or, from the center of the C♮ hole in a B♮ or a B♭ foot-joint] to the face of the cork is 618.5 millimeters, and that the length of the first octave from the center of the hole for C_3 to the center of the hole for C_4 is 335 millimeters; thus the upper portion is 51.5 millimeters shorter than the lower, and in calculating, this quantity (51.5 millimeters) must be taken into consideration. [This quantity may be called the "closed-end correction" for this particular size of tube (see page 42).]

By doubling the length of the octave one obtains as the theoretical air column the length of 670 millimeters, which serves as the unit of calculation, and from which, corresponding to the normal pitch [A=435], are obtained the following absolute vibration-numbers and the relative and the actual length-measures. [All the dimensions in this table and throughout this text, which refer to the positions of tone-holes are measured from the *centers* of the holes. The numbers in this table have been recomputed by the translator. The numbers of vibrations for the tones for the next lower octave are obtained by dividing the numbers in the first column by two, and for the higher octave by multiplying by two; the theoretical lengths of the air column for the next lower octave are obtained from the second column by multiplying by two, and for the higher octave by dividing by two. The actual lengths of air column for other octaves cannot be obtained by this simple process, but must be determined by experiment.]

TABLE II

Tones	Absolute Vibration Numbers	Theoretical Lengths of Air Column	Actual Lengths of Air Column
C_4	517.31	335.00mm	283.50mm
B_3	488.27	354.92	303.42
B_3b $A_3\sharp$	460.87	376.02	324.52
A_3	435.00	398.38	346.88
A_3b $G_3\sharp$	410.59	422.07	370.57
G_3	387.54	447.17	395.67
G_3b $F_3\sharp$	365.79	473.76	422.26
F_3	345.26	501.93	450.43
E_3	325.88	531.78	480.28
E_3b $D_3\sharp$	307.59	563.40	511.90
D_3	290.33	596.90	545.40
D_3b $C_3\sharp$	274.03	632.40	580.90
C_3	258.65	670.00	618.50

Evidently for the practical application, 51.5 millimeters must be subtracted from each of the theoretical lengths to obtain the actual lengths, given in the third column, which determine the distances between the face of the cork and the center points for boring the tone-holes. [See the diagram on page 41.]

[The center of the blow-hole is 17.00 millimeters from the face of the cork. The center of the C_4 hole (the thumb-key hole) is 283.50 millimeters from the cork. The distance of 618.50 millimeters for the C_3 hole is for a lateral tone-hole in a tube which extends downwards to B♮ or lower. If the flute is in C, then this tone is given by the open end. As mentioned on page 29, the distance between the center of the C_3♯ hole and the end of the tube is found by experiment to be 5 millimeters greater than the distance to the center of a hole for C_3 located by the simple theory, hence it follows that the open end for C_3 is $618.50+5.00=623.50$ millimeters from the face of the cork.]

[The center of a tone-hole for C_3 is 618.50 millimeters from the cork. Extending the *Schema*, the distance of the center of a lateral tone-hole for B♮ (foot-joint) is 658.32 millimeters. If this tone is given by the open end, the correction is $+5.30$ millimeters, and the distance of the open end of a B♮ foot-joint is thus 663.62 millimeters from the cork. As mentioned on page 48, Boehm usually made the head-joint about 2 millimeters short at the tuning slide. This should be taken into account when measuring actual flutes.]

[In the system of fingering devised by Boehm, now in general use, the tone F♯ is obtained by pressing down with either the third, or second finger of the right hand, with the result that there is one closed hole below the open hole from which the tone F♯ is being emitted. This closed hole has the effect of slightly lowering the pitch of the tone. To compensate for this flattening the tone-hole for F♯ is usually placed a little above the position indicated in Table II. This displacement is about 1.2 millimeters, which gives 422.26 − 1.20=421.06 millimeters from the cork as the compensated position of the center of the F♯ hole.]

[In order to complete the dimensions of a flute, it is necessary to add data for the upper C♯ hole, and for the trill-key holes for D♮ and D♯. There is no formula for calculating these quantities. A study of ten selected Boehm & Mendler flutes gives the following dimensions:

	Diameter	Distance of center form cork
D♯ trill-key hole	7.6mm	216.30mm
D♮ trill-key hole	7.6	233.40
C♯ small tone-hole	6.6	253.50

Occasionally a flute is found with these small holes of a different diameter, and with corresponding changes in their positions; but the data given represent Boehm's later instruments.]

[The dimensions given in this section correspond to the pitch A=435, and for tone-holes 13.2 millimeters in diameter, having a maximum rise above the edge of the hole of about 3 millimeters; the data for any other pitch may be determined by the method described in the next section.]

III. EXPLANATION OF THE SCHEMA

IN Table II there is given only one set of normal dimensions; since the normal pitch [now known as International or low pitch: A=435] is by no means in universal use, it is often necessary to have measurements corresponding to various given pitches, but the labor required to make the necessary calculations of dimensions involves much time and trouble.

These inconveniences have caused me to design a *Schema* in which the basis of all the calculations for measurements of length is graphically represented. In this diagram the geometrical proportions of the lengths of a string, corresponding to the reciprocals of the vibration numbers in the equally tempered scale, are represented by the intersections of horizontal and vertical lines; while diagonal lines indicate the geometrical progression in which the measures of length may be varied without disturbing their reciprocal proportions to the vibration numbers.

This graphic method was suggested by the plan of a monochord, on which, by means of a moveable bridge, the stretched string may be successively shortened to half of its original length, thereby producing all the intervals of one octave.

Now these proportions remain constant from the highest to the lowest musical tones, and the transition from one interval to the next can therefore be represented graphically, and my *Schema* has been founded upon these considerations. With its help and without calculation, the centers of the tone holes of all wind instruments constructed on my system, as well as the positions of the so-called frets of guitars, mandolins, zithers, etc., may be easily and quickly determined.

[The *Schema* seems to have developed gradually during Boehm's study of the dimensions of the flute. The first definite reference to it is in connection with the London Exhibition of 1862. Mr. Wm. Pole reports (Welch, pp. 154, 157.): "He has sent for exhibition a geometrical diagram, with explanations, by which makers of tubular instruments can, with the greatest readiness and accuracy, construct their instruments according to any of the recognized pitches." Boehm later sent a copy of the *Schema* to the Paris Exposition of 1867, but the jury said they were not competent to decide upon the merits of a production which was scientific rather than artistic. In a letter to Mr. Broadwood, dated November 15, 1868, Boehm says: "At the Paris Exposition, unfortunately, the jurors, being unfamiliar with the subject, declined to go into it; wherefore, at the request of the committee of the Bavarian Polytechnic Society, I had my diagrams published in their *Kunst und Gewerbeblatt.*" The account was given in the *Kunst und Gewerbeblatt,* a periodical published in Munich, in October, 1868, and a copy of the original, in German, is in the translator's collection. A complete English translation of this description of the *Schema* has been given by Mr. Broadwood ("Essay on the Boehm Flute," pages 62-69). The explanation give by Boehm in "Die Flöte und das Flötenspiel," differs from that in the *Kunst und Gewerbeblatt* mainly in the omission of a figure showing details of the diagram; this figure has been reproduced in this edition as Fig. 12. A critical discussion of the *Schema,* as submitted to the Paris Exposition, has been given by M. Cavaillé-Coll (Welch, "History of the Boehm Flute," pages 306-313).]

My diagram, Fig. 12, consists of three parallel, horizontal lines of three different lengths, which start from a common vertical line, and are designated by *A, B,* and *C.* [In the original this diagram is given in half-size scale; it is here reproduced about one-fifth full size. In either case, for actual use, it would need to be redrawn accurately to full size. The dimensions shown on the diagram have been added by the translator, to make the construction plain; all of the dimensions are given in Table II. A portion of the *Schema,* drawn to full size, is shown in Fig. 13, on page 45.]

The central line represents the air column of a cylindrical flute tube, open at both ends, corresponding to the stretched string of the monochord, whose fundamental tone is C_3 of the scale founded on the normal pitch $A_3 = 435$ vibrations. The entire length of this air column, and therefore of the line *B,* for the fundamental tone C_3 is 670 millimeters. The sectional lengths for the tones of the

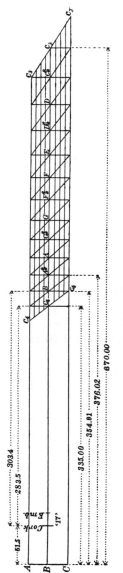

FIG. 12.

Schema for determining the positions of the tone-holes
of wind Instruments at various pitches.

chromatic scale, calculated from the absolute vibration numbers for this pitch, and expressed in
millimeters [see Table II], are given by the points
of intersection of the line *B* with the vertical lines.

There is thus represented a standard of measurement, expressed in millimeters, to be taken from
the upper end of the diagram along the line *B*.
This diagram gives the actual dimensions of my
flute, measured from the cork, if from each relative measure is subtracted the 51.5 millimeters
(represented by the small cross line) which was
previously added to complete the theoretical air
column [see page 34]. More than this, all the
data for calculation are present, if the absolute
vibration numbers are written beneath the points
of intersection of the length measures.

Since these standard measures correspond only
to the normal pitch, it is necessary to be able to
lengthen or shorten the relative distances of the
tone-holes to correspond to varying pitches, with
ease and without disturbing their reciprocal proportions.

This can be accomplished without computation
by means of diagonal lines on the diagram which
pass through the points of intersection of the vertical lines with the line *B*, both upwards and downwards to the points where the vertical lines end
in the two parallel lines *A* and *C*. In this way are
shown two new sets of measures, one corresponding to a pitch a half tone sharper, the other to
one a half tone flatter.

[The construction may be carried out graphically as follows: After the several vertical lines have been drawn through the points of intersection on *B*, the line *A* is drawn parallel to *B* at any convenient distance; a diagonal line is drawn through each intersection of a vertical line with *A* to the intersection of the next lower vertical line with *B*, and is continued until it intersects the second lower vertical line below *B*; the line *C* is then determined by the last intersections of the diagonal and vertical lines.   If these intersections do not all fall on a straight line parallel to *B*, there has been a mistake in the construction of the diagram; as Boehm says, "the accuracy of the drawing is self-controlled."   Obviously, the ratio of the distances between the parallel lines *A*, *B*, and *C*, must be the same as that of the distances between any three successive vertical lines, which is the ratio of the semi-tone intervals of the equally tempered scale, 1.0595.   In Fig. 12, these distances have been taken equal to those between the vertical line for *G* and *F♯*, and *F♯* and *F*, 26.59 millimeters and 28.17 millimeters, respectively. Any other pair of distances between tone-holes, would give a diagram with diagonal lines of a different slope, but all would lead to the same dimensions for the flute.]

A flute made to the shortened measurements of line *A*, will be exactly half a tone sharper than the normal pitch, while one made upon the longer dimensions of line *C*, will be exactly a half tone lower than the normal pitch.   Now as these diagonal lines may be looked upon as continuous series of tone-hole centers, which, in a geometrical progression, gradually approach each other above, and in the same way recede from each other below, it follows that the relative proportions of the distances of these points remain continually unchanged, wherever the diagonal lines are intersected by a new line parallel to the line B.

It is possible, therefore, as shown in the diagram, to draw six additional parallel lines between A and C, which, together with B, will give dimensions differing in pitch by one-eighth of a tone; and at will many other lines may be drawn, the intersections of each of which with the diagonal lines will give correct dimensions. The only remaining question is how such a line shall be drawn so that it shall correspond exactly to any given pitch.

In order to answer this question one must first express the pitch difference between the given pitch and the normal, in millimeters, which will give the difference between the length of the air column of the given tone, and the length for the same tone in normal pitch shown on line B. This will also determine the position of a new vertical section line crossing the line B, corresponding to the given tone.

If the desired pitch is higher than the normal, the vertical section line through the point on line B, corresponding to the new pitch, is to be extended upward toward A; while if the pitch is lower than the normal, the vertical line is to be extended downward toward C.

In either case the intersection of the vertical

line with a diagonal line is the point through which a new line parallel to *B* is to be drawn. The conversion of pitch difference into longitudinal measurement may be carried out as follows. The pitch to which an instrument is to be constructed may be given by a tuning fork, a tuning pipe, or by the number of vibrations, and in the *Schema* either an A or a C may be used.

For example, let there be given by a tuning fork an A_3 of 430 vibrations, which is 5 vibrations flatter than the normal A_3 of 435 vibrations, for which pitch the positions of all the tone-holes are required. In this case it is necessary merely to draw

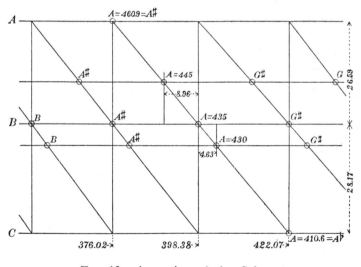

FIG. 13. A portion of the *Schema*.
Full size.

out the head joint of a normal flute until it is exactly in tune with the tuning fork (which naturally the ear determines) in which case the length drawn out will be found to be 4.63 millimeters. If, however, the given pitch is higher than the normal, for example $A_3 = 445$ vibrations, then, since the flute cannot be shortened, the head joint is to be drawn out till the tone B♭ is in unison with the A_3 of the fork. The length drawn out will be found to be 13.40 millimeters; and since the distance between the centers of the B_3♭ and A_3 holes of the normal flute is 22.36 millimeters, it follows that the air column corresponding to the A_3 of the fork is shorter than that of the normal flute by 8.96 millimeters.

If the pitch differences are given by vibration numbers, then the conversion into millimeter measures must be calculated. The vibration numbers are inversely proportional to the lengths; and the vibration numbers $A_3 = 430$ and $A_3 = 445$ are to the normal vibration number $A_3 = 435$, as the relative normal length 398.38 milimeters is to the required lengths. If now the numbers 435 and 398.38 are multiplied together, and the resulting product is divided by the numbers 430 and 445, the quotients are 403.01 and 389.42 which then represent the numbers of millimeters in the relative lengths, to which the vibration numbers have been converted. If these measurements correspond to the given vibration numbers 430 and 445, then the differences between them and the length of the normal A_3, 4.63 and 8.96 millimeters, must correspond to the vibration differences of 5 and 10 vibrations, respectively.

Therefore a vertical section line drawn through the line B at a point 4.63 millimeters distant from the center of the A_3 hole in the direction of $A_3\flat$, will correspond to $A_3=430$ vibrations; and a section line 8.96 millimeters distant from the A_3 hole in the direction of $A_3\sharp$ will correspond to A_3 $=445$ vibrations.

[In Boehm's original description of the *Schema* in the *Kunst und Gewerbeblatt,* a diagram accompanies the preceding explanation, which is omitted in "Die Flöte und das Flötenspiel." This drawing, given in Fig. 13, with some elaboration and with dimensions added, shows a portion of the *Schema* drawn accurately to full scale.]

The desired points of intersection will, in the manner mentioned above, be obtained from the diagonals leading upward or downward, and the results of this method of procedure will be found to be perfectly accurate.

Since the relative proportions of the vibration numbers and the measurements remain unchanged throughout the diagram, it is immaterial whether the given tone is an A, a C, or any other; and if the diagram is not sufficiently long for lower tones, it can be extended at will.

For each successive lower octave one has only to double all the dimensions; the accuracy of the drawing controls itself, for any error made would be at once evident by the drawing of the diagonal lines.

From this explanation it is evident that a flute can be in perfect tune at one pitch only, and that any shortening or lengthening of the tube above the tone-holes must work disadvantageously upon the intonation; in the first case the higher tones as compared with the lower are too sharp, and in the second case [drawing the tuning side], on the contrary, the lower tones are too sharp as compared with the higher.

Obviously, these difficulties are no more overcome by a longer or shorter head-joint, than by a simple drawing of the slide; this drawing-out must not be more than two millimeters. Small differences of pitch can, indeed, be compensated, so far as the ear is concerned, by a good embouchure. Accordingly I make the head-joints of my flutes about two millimeters shorter than is required for perfect tuning, so that one may not only draw out the head to lower the pitch, but that he may also make it somewhat sharper. However, it is best in ordering a flute to specify the pitch as accurately as possible, and at the same time to mention whether the player directs his embouchure inward or outward, as this also produces a considerable effect on the pitch.

[A study of eleven specimens verifies the statement made above. Four of these head-joints are exactly two millimeters short; two of them are three millimeters short. The average amount of shortening is 2.4 millimeters. Unfortunately the variation in pitch within the last fifty years has led many owners of Boehm's flutes to have them purposely altered; and often there are repairs to the head, or slide-joint, which alter the length. No instrument has ever been found which differs from the specified dimensions, which does not also show evidence of having been altered.]

[There has been a great deal of discussion as to the validity and utility of the *Schema*. It has been stated that Boehm himself did not follow the *Schema;* that flute makers in general do not use it; that a flute made according to the *Schema* would be so badly out of tune as to be unusable. (Rockstro, "The Flute," p. 169; Welch, "History of the Boehm Flute," p. 297). Much study has been given to the design of the scale of the flute, involving the accurate measurement of several hundred specimens, among which have been, perhaps, fifty made by Boehm. These flutes by Boehm represent all stages of his work from the year 1850 to 1880, and are of all sizes; there are bass flutes in G, military flutes in Db, orchestra flutes of various pitches, and several with B♮ foot-joints. Every flute from Boehm's shops so far examined has been constructed accurately upon the dimensions explained in connection with the *Schema*. There is little need for argument regarding the tuning of these instruments: for fifty years many of the most eminent artists have used Boehm's flutes in some of the finest orchestras of the world, where the requirements of accurate tuning are the most exacting. At the time of writing (1921) the translator is using a Boehm & Mendler silver flute, made according to the *Schema* for the pitch $A = 435$. This has been played in direct comparison with several other instruments of the very highest quality recently made by the most eminent makers in America and abroad; and also in comparison with a flute constructed upon the translator's own improved (?) scale. Each flute has its individual characteristics, but in general Boehm's *Schema* is fully justified.]

[The *Schema* is certainly based upon rational principles, that is, it is "scientific;" it consists of the application of the laws of the musical scale to quantitive measurements. The fundamental interval of the octave is found only by experiment, and Boehm's value is the result of his years of experience. Any change in the diameter of the bore, in the size of the blow-hole, in the size of the tone-holes, in the length of the tube around the holes; any change in the rise of the keys, in the hardness of the pads, in the diameter of the metal washer holding the pads in place; any change in the manner of blowing, or even in the physical condition of the player himself—any of these changes would alter the fundamental interval and lead to a set of dimensions different from those given by Boehm. Nevertheless, the *Schema* is quite correct for a flute played as Boehm intended it to be played. Many performers wish modifications to favor or correct certain tones, or to suit their personal idiosyncrasies, and makers have adopted such changes, thus departing in detail from Boehm's measures. Such a change may be acceptable to one player and not to another; in any case they do not invalidate the *Schema*. In examining old flutes account must be taken of possible alterations. For instance the Heindl Flute, No. 19, (page 99) has the tone-holes spaced according to the *Schema* for the scale of A=445,

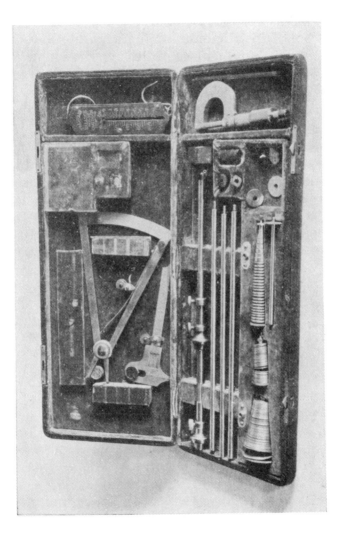

Fig. 14.

A set of instruments designed especially for measuring flutes

but the slide-joint has been shortened by 8 millimeters, raising the pitch to A=452. Evidence of
this change is very plain when looked for.]

[A set of instruments for the accurate and convenient measurement of flutes, is shown in Fig.
14. With the exception of three pieces these tools
were especially made for this purpose. There is a
special caliper for measuring the diameters of the
tone-holes without removing the keys; a jointed
measuring rod, 1000 millimeters long, with vernier
and with a special compensation, adjustable to
any flute so that all measurements of length are
referred to the center of the embouchure; a set
of 170 standard disks for diameters of bore and
of holes, differing by tenths of a millimeter (0.004
inch); a caliper for inside, outside, and depth
measures; a standard micrometer caliper; and a
delicate spring balance for weighing the parts.]

IV. THE MATERIAL

THAT the tones of a flute may not only be easily produced, but shall also possess a brilliant and sonorous quality, it is necessary that the molecules of the flute tube shall be set into vibration at the same time as the air column, and that these shall, as it were, mutually assist one another. The material must possess this requisite vibration ability, which is either a natural property of the body, for example as in bell-metal, glass and various kinds of wood, or has been artificially produced, as in the case of hardened steel springs and hard-drawn metal wire. [Undoubtedly the material of which a wind instrument is made sometimes affects the tone quality, but the manner in which this influence is exerted has not been explained; it is doubtful whether it is correct to ascribe it to the molecular vibrations of the material.]

Now in both cases the excitation of the vibrations requires the expenditure of energy proportional to the mass of the material. Consequently the tones of a flute will be more easily produced and the development of their full strength will require less effort in blowing, the less the weight of the flute tube.

Upon a silver flute, therefore, the thin and hard drawn tube of which weighs only **129 grams,** the brightest and fullest tone can be brought out and maintained much longer without fatiguing blowing, than can be done on a wood flute, which even when made as thin as possible still has double the weight, namely 227½ grams. [The silver tubes used by Boehm have a thickness of about 0.28 millimeters and the wooden tubes are 3.7 millimeters thick. The silver flute complete weighs about 330 grams and the wooden flute about 440 grams.]

Any variation in the hardness or brittleness of the material has a very great effect upon the timbre or quality of tone. Upon this point much experience is at hand, for flutes have been made of various kinds of wood, of ivory, crystal-glass, porcelain, rubber, papier-mâché, and even of wax, and in every conceivable way to secure the various desired results. Heretofore all of these researches have led back to the selection of very hard wood, until I succeeded in making flutes of silver and German silver, which now for twenty years have rivaled the wood flute. [Silver flutes were first introduced by Boehm in 1847.] Notwithstanding this it is not possible to give a decisive answer to the question "Which is the best?"

The silver flute is preferable for playing in very large rooms because of its great ability for tone modulation, and for the unsurpassed brilliancy and sonorousness of its tone. But on account of its unusually easy tone-production, very often it is overblown, causing the tone to become hard and shrill; hence its advantages are fully realized only through a very good embouchure and diligent tone-practice. For this reason wooden flutes on my system are also made, which are better adapted to the embouchures of most flute players; and the wood flutes possess a full and pleasant quality of tone, which is valued especially in Germany.

The silver flutes are made of a $\frac{9}{10}$ fine alloy [United States coin silver is $\frac{9}{10}$ fine; sterling silver is $\frac{925}{1000}$ fine]; and for the manufacture of wood flutes I usually employ either the so-called cocus wood, or the grenadilla wood of South America. The first, of dark or red-brown color, is especially desirable because of its brilliant tone, notwithstanding that this wood contains a resin, which, in very rare cases, induces an inflammation of the skin of the lip. To obviate this difficulty, as well as to secure a very pleasant ringing quality of tone in the high notes, many will prefer black grenadilla wood. Ebony and boxwood are now used only for the cheaper grades of instruments.

In the construction of my flutes only selected wood of the finest quality is used, and if a piece develops a defect during the working, it is at once cast aside, that no more time and labor may be lost.

However, a flute which is entirely free from defects may become cracked by improper handling, against which no guarantee is possible. Both the cause and the means of preventing such accidents should be understood, and I will therefore return to this subject later, under the heading, Treatment of the Flute in General.

[Boehm frequently combined two materials, making the body of silver and the head of wood. It was in his later years that he most strongly advocated this combination, though he had constructed such flutes in his earlier years, certainly as early as 1865. Three such instruments are shown in Figs. 7, 32, and 41; the latter two have heads of "thinned" wood. Notwithstanding Boehm's recommendation, such composite instruments have not grown in favor.]

Yours most truly
Theobald Boehm.

V. THE SYSTEM OF FINGERING

(a) GENERAL DESCRIPTION

H AVING determined the dimensions and material best suited for the flute tube, it was then necessary to devise a system of fingering by which all scales, passages, and trills in the twenty-four keys could be played, clearly, certainly, and with the greatest possible ease. [The chronological order is not accurately stated, for the system of fingering was practically completed in 1832, while the dimensions and material, as described above, were altered by the introduction, in 1847, of the silver flute with cylinder bore.]

This task I endeavored to accomplish in the following manner. Since the fifteen tone-holes of my flute tube could not be covered by means of the fingers, because the holes were too large and in some instances too far apart, it was necessary to furnish them all with keys which had then to be so arranged that they could be opened or closed at will.

For this purpose but nine fingers are available, since the thumb of the right hand is indispensable for holding the flute. The deficiency in fingers must therefore be made up by mechanism, whose systematic coupling makes it possible to close several keys at the same time with one finger. I have accomplished this by means of moveable axles, to which some of the keys are rigidly fastened, and on which other keys are merely hinged; by means of clutches underneath, the latter may be made to act upon the axles.

These axles may be lengthened as desired, so that the attached keys are manipulated at points within easy reach of the fingers; the means for accomplishing this had to be sought in the design of the key mechanism. After mature consideration of all the possible tone combinations and finger movements I made many sketches of mechanisms, in my effort to find the best methods of key connections. In such matters only actual trial can determine which is best. I constructed flutes on three entirely different models and after careful trial of all the advantages and disadvantages, that model of my flute which has since become well known proved itself in all respects the most suitable.

I have retained the three foot keys for C_3♯, D_3, D_3♯, for the little finger of the right hand, in the form already well established. The two trill keys for D_4 and D_4♯ are brought into use only for the highest tones B_5♭ and B_5. Hence the number of keys to be arranged for in the regular scheme of fingering is reduced from fifteen to ten for the playing of which there are still eight fingers available.

There then arose the question, "Which method of construction, that with open keys or that with closed keys, is the most practicable?"

I chose the open keys, as giving the greatest

possible ease in playing, since they easily follow the movement of the fingers, and only weak springs are required to raise them quickly. On the contrary, closed keys require strong springs in order that large holes may be stopped airtight, and their motions are contrary to those of the fingers, [that is, when the finger is pressed downward the key over the hole moves upward].

After the ten holes from E to C♯ were provided with separate, easily moving keys, the eight fingers were placed upon them in the most practical arrangement which permitted the holding of the flute in a natural manner; then as many keys were closed as could be done with entire convenience; there remained open only the two holes for G and B [which, when closed, give F♯ and B♭], and for the closing of these the lack of fingers must be made up by mechanical contrivances.

For this two key combinations were necessary, namely the clutches for connecting the E, F, and F♯ keys with the lengthened moveable axle of the G key, and the clutches of the B♭ and the F♯ keys connecting with the axle of the B key.

As is shown in the following drawing (Fig. 20), the two keys G and B may be closed by means of the connected keys, without changing the lay of the fingers, and when the fingers are lifted the keys open of themselves by means of their own springs; thus one can play them at will.

In this way the very troublesome sliding from keys and tone-holes which is required on the old flute is entirely done away with, and one can certainly and easily play all possible tone combinations from low D_3 to high A_5. In my system each scale requires the use of all the fingers, and consequently they are all equally exercised, thus a player is in a condition to play in all keys with equal accuracy, certainty and ease.

In the following table of fingerings [page 72], those designated "irregular" may be used not only for facilitating certain passages, but they may also be employed in many cases for enharmonic differences, such as between F♯ and G♭.

The practicability of my system of fingering has long demonstrated itself not only in its use by artists, but also by beginning students who learn to play the scales and trills in all keys in much shorter time than was possible on the old flute.

The changing from the old flute to the new is not nearly so difficult as most players imagine. Ordinarily it requires only about two weeks for one to become familiar with the mechanism and the table of fingerings; and one will find compensation for the trouble involved in the clear, smooth and easy production of the tones.

(b)   THE G♯ KEY

In the planning of my system of fingering, I made the G♯ key to stand open, like all the rest, only after mature consideration of all the advantages and disadvantages in acoustical, mechanical, and technical respects. The open key is advantageous because its motion is the same as that of the little finger of the left hand, and because of the weak spring required, its "play" is very light and convenient.

Since the unlearning of the former fingering appears to be a great difficulty to many [who would change from the ordinary flute to the new], artists and instrument makers have endeavored to adapt the fingering of the old flute, either wholly or in part, to my flute tube. For this reason there has been made in Paris, for many years, an alteration of my open G♯ key, which makes it like the closed G♯ key in its action. The use of this has spread somewhat, since it accommodates players of the old flute who can thus retain the former fingerings for G and G♯.

[The earliest type of G♯ key, first applied to the old system flute about 1775, is a simple key which is normally kept closed by a spring; this key is opened by the little finger of the left hand to produce the tone G♯. Boehm's system of 1832 required open keys and he devised the equally simple "Open G♯ Key." The earliest form of this key is shown in Fig. 4. After the invention of the cylinder bore and large, covered keys, in 1847, the key was given the form shown in Fig. 7, the A and G♯ keys being hinged on a short rod on the left (outer) side of the tube. Later all of the mechanism was attached to the inner side of the tube and the G♯ key took its present form as shown in Fig. 16. The A and G♯ keys are independently hinged on a short rod and each is an open-standing key. The third finger of the left hand plays directly on the A key and when the key is closed the tone

G♯ is produced. When the little finger of the left hand is pressed on the lever attached to the G♯ key this key is closed, making the tone G♮. The little finger must continue to close this key for the lower tones, F♯, F, E, etc. With the open G♯ key the little finger is in action to close the key for twenty-one notes of the thirty-nine notes which make the compass of the regular scale. With the closed G♯ key the little finger is required to open the key for five notes out of the thirty-nine notes in the scale. This more frequent use of the little finger, however, is so simple and logical and so directly in accord with the movements of the other fingers, that the open G♯ system, when once acquired, is quite as easy as any other.]

[Coche, of Paris, a teacher of the flute, brought out in 1838 the "Coche Perfected Model" which he announced as an improvement upon the Boehm system. One of the "improvements" was the adoption of a new type of closed G♯ key, devised about this time by Dorus, another flutist of Paris. A conical-bore flute by Godfroy, shown in Fig. 6, is provided with a Dorus G♯ key of the early form. This type of key as applied to the cylinder-bore flute of later type is shown in Fig. 17, as made by Louis Lot, and Fig. 15 is a diagram illustrating its operation. There is but one G♯ tone-hole which is opened and closed automatically with the A hole. When the A hole is closed, and with it the G♯ hole, the latter may be independently opened by pressing upon the G♯ lever with the little finger of the left hand. There is a lug, *l*, attached to the hinge tube of the A key which extends under the

stem of the G♯ key; a strong spring, s_1, attached to
the G♯ key rests against the under side of the lug
so that the two keys move together, while,
normally, both are held open by the weak spring,
s_2. The adjustment of the key is such that when the
A key is pressed to close its hole, the G♯ key
touches the flute first; a slight further pressure
of the A key closes the A hole and carries the

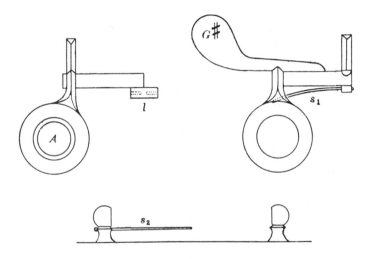

FIG. 15. The Dorus Closed G♯ Key.

lug below the stem of the G♯ key so that the strong
spring, s_1, firmly closes the G♯ hole. While the
A key is held closed by the third finger, and the
G♯ key is closed by the spring, the little finger
may be pressed upon the G♯ lever and thus open
the G♯ hole, producing the tone G♯ as in the old
system. When the little finger is raised the G♯
key closes, making G♮; when the third finger is

raised both keys rise together through the action of the lug and the tone A is produced. This type of key operates satisfactorily on a flute with conical bore and small tone-holes, but on a flute of cylinder-bore and large holes the proper closing of the key is more difficult. The Dorus construction requires the location of the posts and hinge-tubes on the outer side of the flute.]

[The operation of the Dorus G♯ key is not always satisfactory and the necessity of placing the posts and axles of the keys on the outer side of the tube is particularly objectionable on flutes with cylindrical bore and large tone-holes. The Dorus key has largely been displaced by the duplicate-hole, closed G♯ key, Fig. 18, now in very general use. The G♯ tone-hole is placed on the inner side of the flute tube and is covered with a closed key, the manipulation of which is like that of the old system. In order that there may be no closed holes below the one from which the tone is being emitted, a duplicate G♯ tone-hole is used, located as in Boehm's construction; this is closed by a key rigidly attached to the A key; thus the duplicate hole opens and closes with the A hole, and G♯ is produced by pressing on the G♯ key. For certain tones it is desirable to close the G♯ hole while the A hole remains open. This is not possible with the closed G♯ key.]

[Boehm is said to have declined to make flutes with the closed G♯ key. However, he did in a few instances provide such instruments for players of the old flute. The translator has never

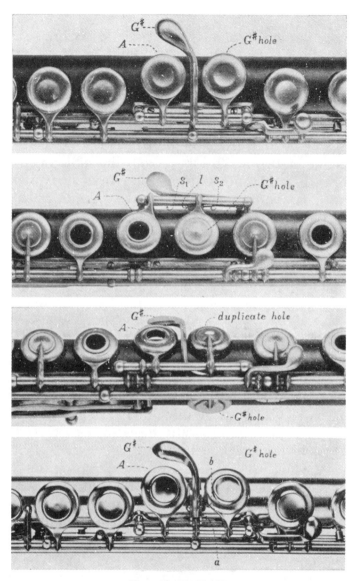

FIGS. 16, 17, 18, 19.
Open and closed G♯ keys

seen but one closed G♯ key made in Boehm's shop; nearly all the closed keys found on these flutes have been added by other makers. The one exception is the Macauley flute shown in Fig. 34. The closed key proper is exactly like Boehm's open G♯ key excepting that the spring is made strong and is so bent that it keeps the key closed. The lever is cut in two a little way from the axle as shown at *a*, Fig. 19, and the finger piece is then pivoted on a fulcrum, *b*, held in a silver guide attached to the tube. This key is played exactly as is the ordinary closed G♯ key; it can be opened and closed independently of the A key; thus it obviates the objections which Boehm urges against the other forms of closed key. Inasmuch as this key is normally closed, it would tend to flatten the tone A, just as the tone F♯ is flattened by the closing of a lower tone-hole. Boehm has corrected this effect upon the tone A by placing the A hole 1.2 millimeters above its *Schema* position, just as he and other makers correct the F♯ tone-hole. This plan of Boehm's is probably the simplest and perhaps the best form of closed G♯ key which has yet been made.]

[Various other schemes for a closed G♯ key have been devised but they are more or less complicated and have not found general acceptance. Boehm's arguments regarding the advantages of the open-key system are given in the following paragraphs.]

A combination of a closed G♯ key with an open A key would cause not only an entirely unnecessary complication in the key mechanism, and be a disadvantage from an acoustical aspect, but it would at the same time increase the difficulties of playing.

In order that a closed G♯ key may stop the large tone-hole air tight it must be provided with a strong spring, and it follows that the opening of the same requires a correspondingly greater force in the little finger of the left hand, than the pressing down of an open key which is held up only by a weak spring. But of still greater importance is the strength required in the third or ring finger in closing the A key, since this finger must overcome not only the spring required quickly to raise both of the combined keys, but at the same time it must overcome the strong closing-spring of the G♯ key. [The last sentence applies only to the Dorus G♯ key.]

It is easily seen that there is thus a loss in facility of playing in general, and, further, that all trills with these keys, and especially the trill G♯ with A, become much more difficult, than with the easy-moving, open-standing keys. Moreover, in the frequent combinations of the tones G♯ or A♭ with the lower tones F♯, F, E, E♭, and D, the little finger of the left hand must move in a direction contrary to that in which the fingers of the right hand are moving at the same time. That it is easier to make similar motions with the fingers of both hands simultaneously, rather than contrary motions, and therefore that playing with a closed G$\sharp$ key is the more difficult, no one will deny.

Yet there is another difficulty from an acoustical aspect. Because of the connection of the G$\sharp$ key with the A key, the A hole cannot be opened by itself, the G$\sharp$ hole being always open at the same time; this causes the E_5 to be too sharp, and its production is interfered with. The production of this tone is a little more certain, when the G$\sharp$ hole remains closed; and in rapid alternations, also in delicate slurring together of the E_5 with other tones such as $G_4\sharp$, A_4, A_5, A_3, etc., the advantage is very perceptible.

Finally, this complication of the mechanism [for any type of closed G$\sharp$ key] is wholly superfluous, since each one of these two keys has its own proper finger, and each can be easily opened or closed in the most natural and simplest way in my system. The above mentioned difficulties appear to have long been apparent in Paris, since a special lever has been added so that the difficult trills may be made with the strong first finger of the right hand.

And yet again a second G$\sharp$ hole has sometimes been bored in the flute tube and provided with an independent G$\sharp$ key. In both of these cases the mechanism is rendered still more complicated. I have no objection to make, if amateurs, with little time or zeal for practice, and who will be satisfied with playing in a few keys only, when changing from the old flute to the new, believe they will find the closed G$\sharp$ key the easier; yet

I hold that it is wrong to instruct beginners in this way, since they will learn to play in all keys more easily, and consequently more quickly, by following my system as finally perfected.

[Rockstro, in his "Treatise on the Flute," pages 191, 359, and 389, argues eloquently and at length in favor of the open G♯ key; he says: "Not many years ago some opposition was raised to the frequent use of the left thumb on the flute. We do not now hear much of this * * * but there is still rife, in some quarters, a strong prejudice against the use of the little finger of the same hand * * *. No one has ever objected to the continued use of the right little finger * * *. Theobald Boehm deserved much credit for his courageous and persistent efforts to bring this finger into activity. * * *"]

[The translator first learned to play a flute of the old-system and then for ten years he used a Boehm system flute with closed G♯ key; later several flutes with open G♯ keys were added to his collection and for the last twenty years he has played mostly upon these. After many years of experience, during which excellent flutes of all three types of G♯ keys were constantly in his possession, and after the most careful and long continued trials, he is firmly convinced that Boehm's arguments are fully justified. The advantages of the open G♯ key are largely mechanical, and may not be sufficient to justify an established performer in changing, but they are such that every beginner and everyone changing from the old to the Boehm system, should choose the open G♯ key.]

VI. TABLES OF FINGERINGS

REGULAR FINGERINGS
OF THE CHROMATIC SCALE
FOR THE NEWLY CONSTRUCTED FLUTE OF
THEOBALD BOEHM

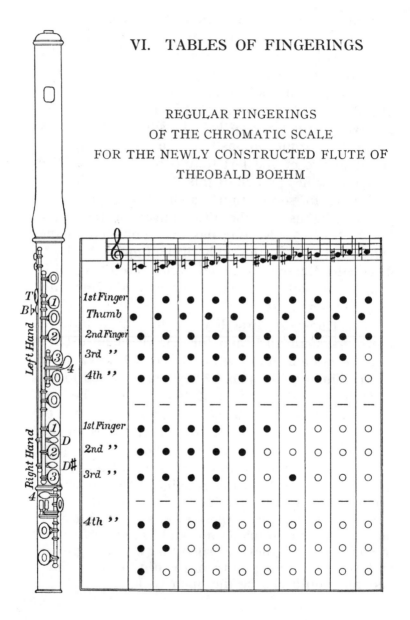

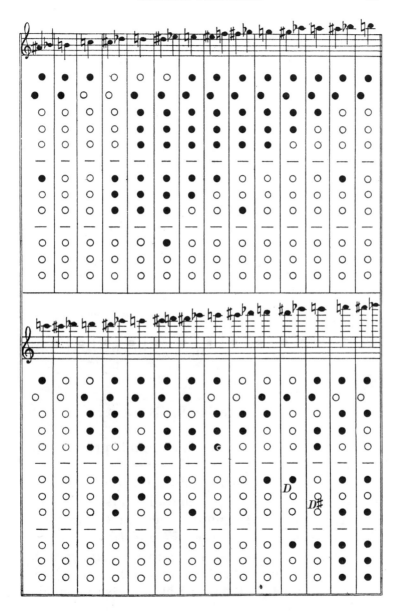

For facility in playing, the two B♭s

can be taken with fingering for B♮.

if the B key is closed by the thumb pressing on the B♭ lever.

The irregular fingerings may be used not only for facilitating certain passages, but also they may be made valuable in many cases for enharmonic differences, such as between F♯ and G♭.

[The use of the octave-key on the ordinary flute is the same as with the bass flute, which is explained on pages 128 and 129; see also page 86.]

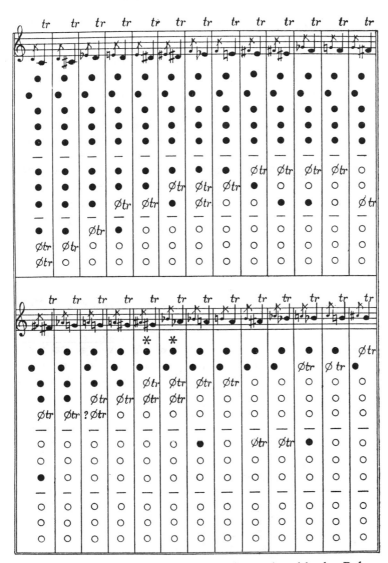

The trills marked with a * are to be made with the B key closed by the thumb lever. [The ? indicates that the trilling of the corresponding hole is optional.]

The trills marked with a * are to be made with the **B key** closed by the thumb lever. [The ? indicates that the trilling of the corresponding hole is optional.]

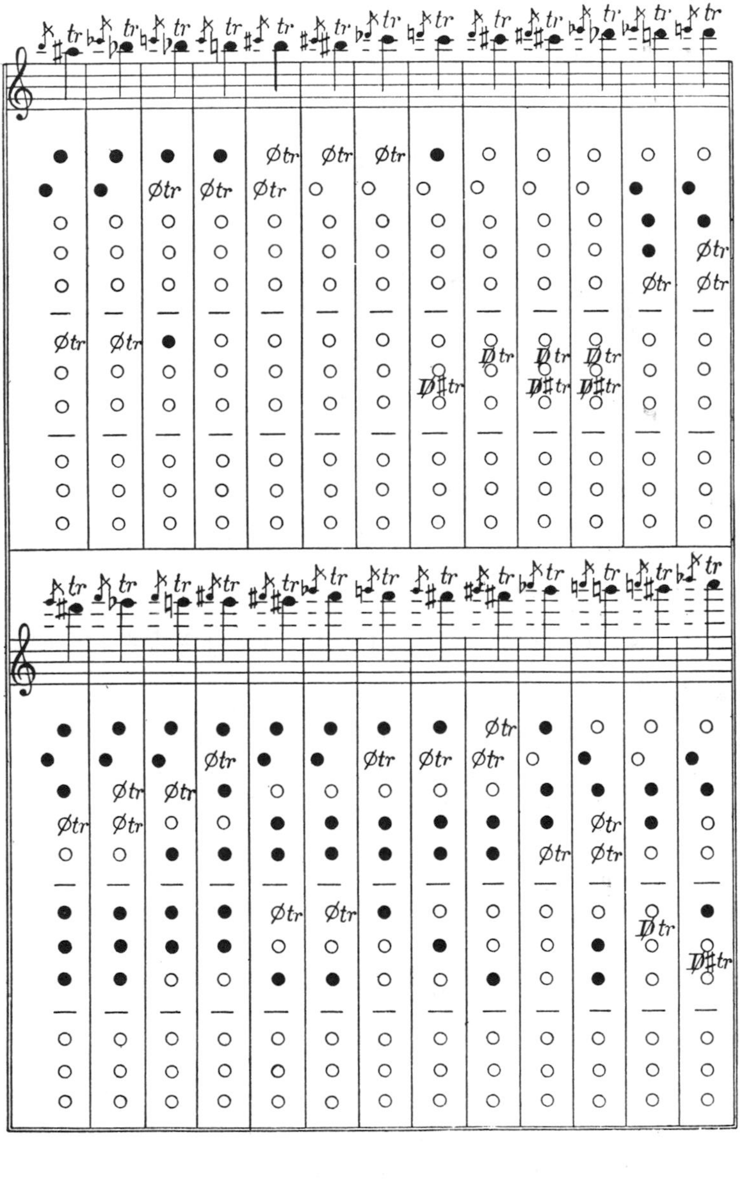

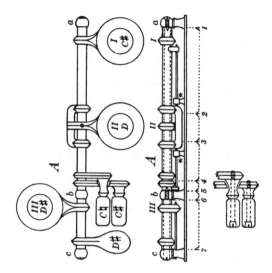

Fig. 20.　Key Mechanism.

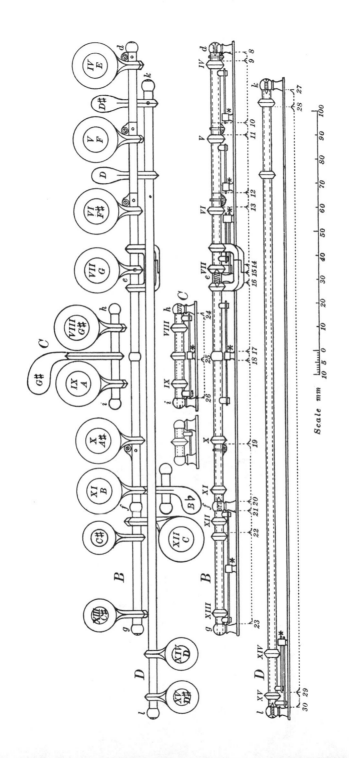

Scale mm

VII. DESCRIPTION OF THE KEY MECHANISM

I N order to give a clear idea and explanation
of the key mechanism of my flute, I have
represented it in full size,* Fig. 20, projected on
a plane, and below I have shown a side view of
the inner parts which are not visible to the eye.

In the latter view metal strips are shown, which
in the metal flute are soldered to the body, and
in the wooden flute are screwed on, forming the
supporting points for the mechanism. Below
these strips, and exactly corresponding with the
drawing above, are dotted lines and figures which
indicate all the joints of the mechanism, and the
dimensions of the axles of the separate keys and
clutches.

The key mechanism is divided into four groups
which are designated in Fig. 20 by *A, B, C,* and *D.*
Fig. 21 is a cross section of one key, Fig. 22 is a

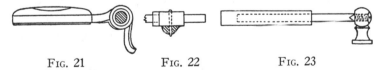

FIG. 21   FIG. 22   FIG. 23

Details of Key Mechanism.

clutch with its pin, and Fig. 23 represents one of
the movable hinge tubes slipped off from its axle.

We will first explain the mechanism of the key-
group *A* of the drawing.

---

* In this Dover edition, Figure 20 is reproduced at a reduction of
approximately 35 per cent.

In the upper line the foot keys I, II, and III are represented, and in the side view beneath, the separate joints of the mechanism are shown, the lengths of which are indicated by the perpendicular dotted lines below the metal strip, designated by the figures 1 to 7.

The three pillars with spherical heads, *a, b, c,* which form the supporting points of the mechanism, are united to the metal strip and soldered, while the strip is soldered or screwed onto the foot joint.

Pointed screws are threaded in the spheres *a* and *b,* forming the pivots on which turns a steel axle (from 1 to 5) the ends of which have conical holes.

The C♯ key, I, turns upon this axle; this key is soldered to the hinge tube 1 to 2, and by means of a loop it connects with the hinge 3 to 4 which carries the lever arm (C♮ lever), all being joined into one continuous piece. The D key II is likewise soldered to a hinge (2 to 3) and being placed inside of the loop, the two keys are slipped over the axle; the key II is then made fast to the axle by a small pin passing through both. On the upper end of the axle (at 4 to 5) a lever arm is soldered, so that the axle and the D key move with it. These two keys are provided with springs which hold them open, and with rollers screwed onto the lever arms at right angles; by pressing on the rollers one can at will close one key, or through their coupling at the loop, both may be closed together.

The closed D♯ key III is provided with a strong spring, and moves on an axle, screwed into the sphere *b;* the sharpened end of this axle (at 5) forms the pivot of the movable axle of the lower keys.

The springs for the keys I and II are firmly inserted in the little posts marked thus, *, and push against the hinges by means of small blocks which are soldered fast; the spring for key III is fastened in the spherical pillar *c.*

The key-group *B* contains two moveable axles from 8 to 15 and from 16 to 20. The G key VII is soldered to the axle, at 14 and 15, which turns on the pivots of the pillars *d* and *e.* Next to this key is the hinge tube 13-14 to which the F♯ key VI and a half of the loop clutch is soldered.

The other half of the loop is fastened to the second moveable axle, and since the two half-loops touch one another, the two moveable axles may be coupled together.

This F♯ key is played by the first or index finger of the right hand.

Next to this is the small hinge piece 12-13, which is fastened to the steel axle by means of a small pin. On this hinge piece there is soldered a side wing, against which presses an adjustable screw attached to the shank of key VI. This screw must be so adjusted that when pressing down the F♯ key VI the steel axle is turned and through this the attached key G VII is closed.

If now the two other keys F V and E IV, which are played by the second and third fingers, are

mounted in exactly the same fashion and are
each coupled with the steel axle, then by pressing
down either of these keys, separately or together,
the G key VII will be closed each time [producing
the tone F♯]; thus four keys and consequently four
tone-holes can be opened or closed at will by three
fingers.   It is by this contrivance that one of the
lacking fingers is replaced.   [The arrangement,
however, is not perfect, for the hole next below
that from which the tone is being emitted is closed.
This lowers the pitch perceptibly and muffles the
tone very slightly.   A partial compensation is
obtained by placing the tone-hole for F♯ slightly
above its true position, as explained on page 37.]

   We come now to the upper half of this group.

   Upon the steel axle which turns between the
two pivots at 16 and 20 there is soldered a hinge,
which extends from 16 to 18 and upon which at
16 there is the half loop for coupling with the
lower steel axle, and at 17 and 18 is attached a
sphere which serves as an ornament.

   The A♯ key X is soldered to the hinge tube 18-19,
and placed next to this sphere. This key is played
by the middle finger of the left hand, and by
means of its adjusting screw presses upon the
wing of the hinge 19-20, through which the B
key XI is closed.

   Since the B key XI is connected to the steel axle
by a pin near 19, and is coupled at 19 with the
A♯ key X by the clutch, and at the same time it is
coupled with the lower steel axle by the loop at
14-15, this key is itself closed by each pressing of

the A♯ key X and also by pressing the F♯ key VI. It is clear that by these couplings still another finger is replaced, and consequently by means of this mechanism [together with that described in the next two paragraphs] six keys can be played entirely at will by four fingers [and the thumb].

Into the upper side of the spherical pillar *f* is screwed an axle, the point of which forms the pivot at 20. Moving on this axle are the two keys C XII and C♯ XIII. The first is soldered to the hinge tube 21-22 and is played by the thumb of the left hand. The second key C♯ XIII, and its lever are soldered to the hinge tube 22-23; the key played by the first or index finger of the left hand acting on the lever.

The group *C* consists of two separate keys, which move on the axle screwed into the spherical pillar *h*. The G♯ key VIII and its lever, upon which presses the fourth or little finger of the left hand, are soldered to the hinge 24-25. The A key IX which is played by the third finger, is soldered to the hinge tube 25-26.

The group *D* likewise contains only two keys, namely the two trill keys for D and D♯. The D♯ key XV and its spring hook are soldered to the hinge tube 29-30, and this tube in turn is soldered to the upper end of the long steel axle which turns on the pivots of the two spherical pillars *k* and *l*. On the lower end of this axle is the short piece of tube 27-28, which is connected with the axle by a pin; soldered to this tube is the D♯ lever which is played by the third finger of the right hand.

Between these two pieces is placed a long hinge tube which reaches from 28 to 29. Upon the upper end is soldered the D key XIV and at the lower end the corresponding D lever, which is played by the second finger. Both keys are provided with strong closing springs at 29 and 30.

Besides these keys there is still to be provided a B♭ lever next to the C key XII, which can be pressed with the thumb of the left hand, at the same time that the C key is closed, thus closing the B key XI also [and producing the tone B♭]. This lever is provided with its axle and spring, and serves in many cases to facilitate the playing.

Further, as the drawings show, all the springs, with the exception of that for closing the lower D♯ key III [and for the B♭ thumb lever], are fastened in the little pillars designated with an *; these springs press upon little hooks soldered to the hinge tubes, in such a way as to close the two trill keys D and D♯, and to hold all the other keys open.

These explanations correspond to all the styles of flutes made by the firm "Th. Boehm & Mendler in München."

[The original Boehm-system flute, including the models both of 1832 and of 1847, did not have a B♭ thumb lever. This attachment was devised by Briccialdi, an Italian flutist then resident in London, and was first applied to his own flute by Rudall and Rose in 1849. This lever, essentially in its original form, marked *B♭* in Figs. 24 and 26, is in very general use at the present time. Soon

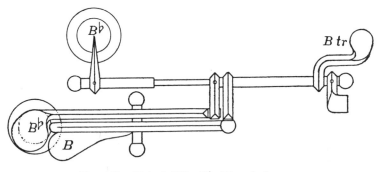

FIG. 24. Briccialdi's B♭ Thumb Levers.

after Briccialdi's invention, Boehm devised the B♭ thumb lever described in the preceding paragraph and marked *B♭*, in Figs. 25, 27 and 28.]

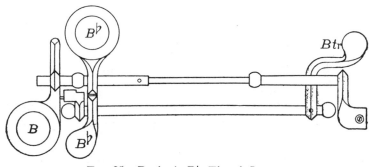

FIG. 25. Boehm's B♭ Thumb Levers.

[A lever for making the trill of B and C, *B tr* in Figs. 24, 25, 26 and 27, played with the first finger of the right hand, has been combined with each of these arrangements. Boehm seems never to have considered these levers as essential parts of his system, but rather as extra attachments; this is indicated by the fact that they are used only incidentally in the Tables of Fingerings. Boehm considered his own arrangement more rational than that of Briccialdi, since the thumb is placed on the key *B*, Figs. 25, 27 and 28, to produce the tone B, and to produce the next *lower* tone B♭, the thumb is moved *downwards* to the lever *B♭*. On the contrary, in Briccialdi's arrangement, the thumb is placed on *B*, Figs. 24 and 26, to produce the tone B, and to produce the *lower* tone B♭, the thumb is moved *upwards* to the lever B♭.]

[In addition to the mechanism described, Boehm recommended the "Schleifklappe," referred to in the original only in connection with the Bass Flute. The schleif-key, usually called the "octave-key" or the "whisper-key," is simply a small vent-key, which assists in the formation of a loop in the sound wave, or, what is of the same effect, it prevents the formation of a node at the place where the hole is located, thus giving freer speech and greater purity of tone. It is an adaptation of a similar octave-key which is required on all reed instruments, in which the formation of the over-tones is not as certain as on the flute. The octave-key is a small closed key, the touch of which is at *S*, Figs. 27 and 28, just above the thumb key; it is always played in connection with the thumb key and is easily opened by a slight rolling motion of the thumb. The hole for this key on a C flute is from 4.5 to 5.0 millimeters in diameter and is placed about 7 millimeters above the C♯ hole. The applications of the fingerings for the flute, in C are the same as for the bass flute, which are

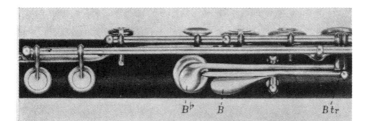

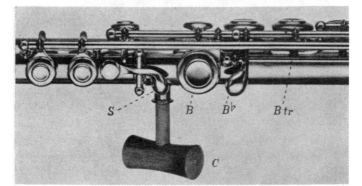

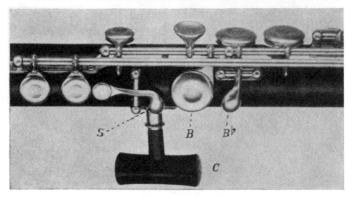

FIGS. 26, 27, and 28.
Briccialdi and Boehm thumb keys

given in the supplementary tables of fingerings on page 129. Boehm writes in a letter dated November 8, 1873 (Broadwood, p. 59): "I find this little key very useful if the player wishes always to be in perfect tune in the following notes:

These tones always have a tendency to get a little flat if played *pianissimo,* while if you open the little octave-key they are not only perfectly correct, but also sound very easily."]

[In the translator's collection are several Boehm & Mendler flutes having the octave-key, one of them being the bass flute in G. After many trials extending over a period of years the conclusion is that, for several of the notes mentioned in the supplementary tables of fingerings, the influence of the key cannot even be detected, while for the other notes its effect is very small, so small as to be entirely negligible. This, no doubt, accounts for the fact that the octave key has not been generally adopted.]

[Fig. 29 is a plan, drawn full size, of the keys for a foot-joint to B♮, as often made by Boehm & Mendler. The action of the low B♮ key is carried around the C♮ and C♯ keys, and is pivoted on an extension of the axle which passes through the D♯ key. The other details are the same as explained for the C♮ foot-joint.]

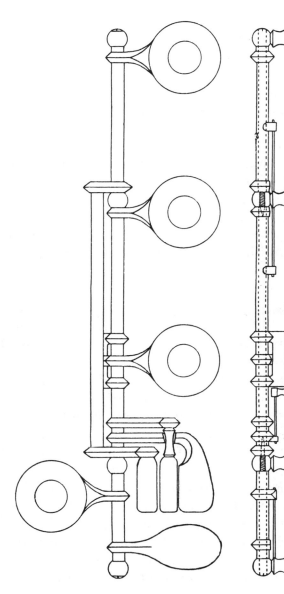

FIG. 29. Mechanism for foot-joint to B.

[The mechanism is substantially the same for flutes of both wood and silver. The walls of the tube of the wooden flute are 3.7 millimeters thick, and the silver tubes are about 0.3 millimeter thick. The "straps," or action plates to which the posts are attached are about 1.2 millimeters thick. The centers of the spherical heads of the action posts, that is the points of the pivot-screws, are about 6.1 millimeters above the plate for the main body and foot-joint keys of a wooden flute, and 6.9 millimeters high for trill keys. For a silver flute the pivots on the body joint are about 8.2 millimeters above the action plate, and on the foot-joint 6.2 millimeters above the action plate. The posts for the A and G♯ keys and for the thumb keys are shorter and vary somewhat in different specimens.]

[From 1812 to 1817 Boehm had a goldsmith's shop in which he constructed flutes on the old system. In 1828, he established his first real flute shop where he made improved old-system flutes and where he worked out the ideas for the Boehm System of fingering which were embodied in the first properly so-called Boehm flute of 1832. Very few flutes were made after 1832 and the shop was entirely given up in 1839. During this period the genuine Boehm flutes were made by Rudall and Rose in London and by Godfroy in Paris, under specific arrangements with Boehm. In 1847 Boehm announced the new flute with cylinder bore, metal body and covered keys, and he again established his own factory for the manufacture of flutes which continued in the same place for over fifty years. (See the appendix.) Patents were obtained in England and France covering the cylinder bore and the parabolic head-joint, and the above-mentioned firms were given licenses to make Boehm flutes. The flutes made in Boehm's own shops from 1847 to 1867 were marked "Th. Boehm in München," and bore serial numbers. In 1854 Carl Mendler, a watchmaker, became a workman in Boehm's shop. In 1862 he was made foreman and he was made a partner in 1867, the firm being known as "Th. Boehm & Mendler." The flutes were marked with the firm name in two styles, as shown in Fig. 30; silver flutes have the name engraved on the barrel of the slide-joint; wooden flutes are marked on a silver ferrule on the tenon of the slide-joint, which is usually covered by the socket on the head-joint. The name is not repeated on other parts of the flute. There are no serial numbers. After Boehm's death, in 1881, the business was carried on by Carl Mendler but the flutes continued to be marked Boehm & Mendler. Carl Mendler was succeeded by his son Carl Mendler, about 1895, who later gave up the manufacture of flutes.]

[Under Mendler's direction the flutes of Boehm & Mendler were constructed with workmanship of the most excellent quality, rarely equalled; they were beautifully designed, exquisitely finished, and their adjustment was perfect. The translator's historical collection of flutes contains, in January, 1922, about two hundred and fifty in-

FIGS. 30.
The Boehm & Mendler labels

struments of all types. Among them are sixteen specimens of various styles and scales from Boehm's own work-shop; these flutes are shown in the group picture, Fig. 31. Three particularly fine instruments, Nos. 13, 5 and 12, which were made for Rev. Rush R. Shippen, Mr. Carl Wehner, and General Daniel Macauley, respectively, are shown in larger size in Figs. 32, 33 and 34. The Heindl flute, No. 9, and the bass flute, No. 16, are shown in Figs. 7 and 41, respectively. These flutes, and also many others of Boehm's make, have been studied critically and have been measured in minute detail. These investigations have developed the greatest admiration for the painstaking care in the details of the scales, for the superb workmanship, and for the exquisite finish of these instruments. The Macauley flute (No. 12 in the group) fully exemplifies this praise. With the exception of the first instrument, which was never furnished with keys, and number nine, the Heindl flute, which has had excessive wear, these flutes are in good order; in fact, most of them are in as perfect condition as when new. The flutes 10, 12, 14 and 16 in the group, are much used for musical purposes, with perfect satisfaction. Some details regarding the several instruments are given in the following list:

No. 1—Flute in G. A=440. Boxwood. Tube of thinned wood with raised finger-holes, to which keys have never been attached. Given by Boehm to James S. Wilkins, Jr., in 1873, and presented to the translator by Mr. Wilkins in 1909.

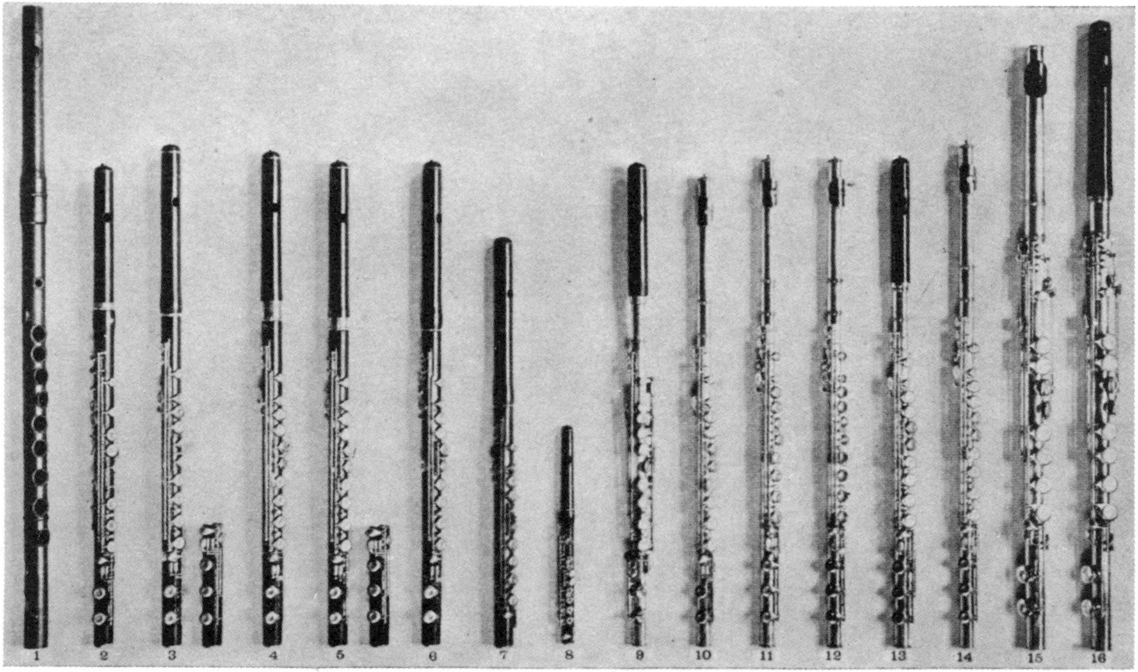

Fig. 31.

Boehm & Mendler Flutes in the Collection of Dayton C. Miller

No. 2—Flute in C. A=450. Grenadilla wood. Silver keys, gold springs. Mechanism of an unusual type, made by Boehm about 1860. Brought to America by Gustave Oeschsle, in 1864, who used it in the New York Academy of Music and in Gilmore's Band. It was later used by Mr. H. H. Honeyman.

No. 3—Flute in C. A=440. Grenadilla wood. Silver keys, gold springs. This flute was obtained from Boehm by Mr. Edward Martin Heindl. It was used by Mr. Frank Wadsworth, and later for eleven years by Mr. Louis Fritze, in Sousa's Band, and played in the "around-the-world" tour. The B♮ foot-joint was used by Mr. William Schade.

No. 4—Flute in C. A=435. Grenadilla wood. Silver keys, steel springs. History unknown.

No. 5—Flute in C. A=445. Cocus-wood. Silver keys, gold springs. With extra foot-joint to B♮. Belonged to Mr. Carl Wehner. Shown separately in Fig. 33.

No. 6—Flute in C. A=450. Cocus-wood. Silver keys, gold springs. With the octave key. With a duplicate-hole G♯ key, added by Wm. R. Meinell. History unknown.

No. 7—Flute in D♭. A=450. Grenadilla wood. Silver keys, gold springs. Foot to D♮.

No. 8—Piccolo in D♭. A=450. Grenadilla wood. Silver keys, steel springs. Cylinder bore. Used by Edward Martin Heindl.

No. 9—Flute in C. A=445. German Silver, silver plated. With graduated tone-holes. No. 19, made by Boehm about 1850. Brought to America in 1864 by Edward Martin Heindl, and used by him in the famous Mendelssohn Quintette Club, and in the Boston Symphony Orchestra upon its organization in 1881. This is probably the first metal Boehm flute to be brought to America. It is provided with both silver and wood heads. The mechanism on the middle joint has been partly rebuilt. This flute originally had no B♭ thumb key, and a special attachment for this was added by Mr. George W. Haynes in 1886, who also used the flute for a time. Shown separately in Fig. 7.

No. 10—Flute in C. A=438. Silver. Gold embouchure, steel springs. The trill lever for the right, first finger operates on the B♮ key on the upper side of the flute, instead of on the thumb key. This flute was played in Buffalo Bill's Wild West Show on its European Tour, and later was used by Mr. W. H. Guyon.

No. 11—Flute in C. A=448. Silver. Gold embouchure, gold springs, octave key, foot-joint to B♮. Made in 1877 for Mr. O. F. Chaffee of Detroit.

No. 12—Flute in C. A=445. Silver. Two sizes of tone-holes. Gold embouchure, gold springs, raised gold plates in center of each key, gold ferrules and tips; octave key, and special form of closed G♯ key (see page 68), ivory crutch. This superb flute is a remarkably beautiful specimen of flute workmanship, and it is in a perfect state of preservation. It was made in 1877, and was on exhibition in Berlin and in Paris for some time (probably in the Paris Exposition of 1878). It was made upon order for General Daniel Macauley, at one time Mayor of Indianapolis. The delivery of the flute was delayed nearly a year, while it was being exhibited. Boehm wrote, in sending the flute, that it was "the last flute I shall ever make and the best I have ever made; it is the 'last child of my life' with which I hate to part." Shown separately in Fig. 34.

No. 13—Flute in C. A=450. Silver. Bore 20 millimeters. Holes spaced to the scale A=455, but sounding A=450 because of the large bore. Two sizes of holes. Head of thinned wood, octave key, gold springs; foot-joint to B♮. Made in 1879 for Rev. Rush R. Shippen. Shown separately in Fig. 32.

No. 14—Flute in C. A=435. Silver. Gold embouchure, gold springs, octave key, foot-joint to B♮. This flute evidently was made about the year 1877. It is in as perfect condition as when new, and is used by the translator for musical purposes perhaps more than is any other instrument in his collection. While it may be equalled as to musical qualities by two or three

FIG. 32.
The Shippen Flute

FIG. 33.
The Wehner Flute

FIG. 34.
The Macauley Flute

modern instruments of the most celebrated makes, yet it is not surpassed by any, and the same may be said with respect to the beauty of design and perfection of workmanship of the instrument as a whole.

No. 15—Flute in G. A=443. Silver. Ebonite embouchure, octave key, steel springs.

No. 16—Flute in G. A=440. Silver. Thinned-wood head, octave key, steel springs. Used by Carl Wehner. Shown separately in Fig. 41. A more complete description with dimensions, is given in Chapter XII.]

[Statements have frequently been made by both makers and players of the flute that Boehm's own instruments were not accurate in scale and were not in accordance with his published descriptions. Such opinions are explicitly stated by Rockstro in his "Treatise on the Flute." This remarkable and otherwise excellent work is sadly marred by the author's intense prejudice against Boehm and by his efforts to belittle Boehm's contributions. Rockstro makes certain specific statements about Boehm's flutes which must be in error. He illustrates and describes a flute made by Boehm, (pages 374, 375, 390, 391) of which he says: "The diameter of the holes of a German silver flute that he made about the year 1851 vary, very irregularly from 0.46 inch (11.7 mm.) for the C_4 hole to 0.539 inch (13.7mm.) for $D_3\sharp$ hole. The distances between the holes are also extremely irregular, so much so that I have not thought it worth while to give an account of them. The tone of this flute is very poor and thin, not nearly equal to that of an eight-keyed flute of average excellence." Nothwithstanding Rockstro's measures are given to the thousandth of an inch, yet it is believed that his general statement must be in error. In support of this opinion, and in justice to Boehm, certain even more specific statements of facts may be made regarding the Heindl flute, Boehm's No. 19 made about 1850, and illustrated as No. 9 in the group picture, and also in Fig. 7. No. 19 is apparently exactly like the flute illustrated in Rockstro's Treatise. No. 19 has graduated holes, the thumb-key hole is 11.4 millimeters in diameter, and the low C♯ hole is 13.6 millimeters in diameter. The holes increase in diameter, with perfect regularity from the smaller to the larger, each hole being exactly 0.2 millimeter larger than the preceeding one. The holes are spaced with perfect regularity, and exactly to the scale A=445, no hole deviating from the precise position required by Boehm's *Schema* by so much as half of a hundredth of an inch (there being the usual correction for the F♯ hole). The fact that Heindl used this flute for solo playing with the famous Mendelssohn Quintette Club and with the Boston Symphony Orchestra for many years is sufficient argument as to its quality of tone and correctness of tuning.]

VIII. CARE OF THE MECHANISM

(a) Repairs

EVEN though kept from violent injuries, the flute, like other mechanisms, will occasionally need repairs.

In practical use the keys move up and down a countless number of times, and all metal being subject to wear, the appearance of defects from this cause is unavoidable, even in the most solidly constructed mechanisms.

A spring may break or lose its elasticity; the oil, with which the axles and pivots must be covered, will become thick and sticky with time, and especially by the entering of dust, thus hindering the easy movement of the keys; or it may be necessary to replace an injured pad.

In all these cases it is necessary to remove the keys from the body and sometimes to take the mechanism to pieces. A person with some experience who has made himself familiar with the construction, and who is provided with the few tools which are required, will have no difficulty in doing this. Every flutist should be in a position, therefore, himself to undertake small repairs, and he should not trust his instrument to incapable hands.

(b) The Keys

The unscrewing and taking apart of the key mechanism may be performed in the manner described in the following paragraphs.

First, all of the springs, designated by a *, Fig. 20, in each key group in which one or more keys are to be taken away, must be unhooked. This may be accomplished by means of the little fork represented in Fig. 35, with which the outer ends

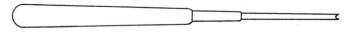

FIG. 35.   Fork for setting springs.

of the springs can be pushed far enough backwards to disconnect them from the little hooks.

For removing the foot keys of group *A*, Fig. 20, turn the pointed screw *a* backwards so that the steel axle with the C♯ I and D II keys attached can be taken out. A screwdriver of the form shown in Fig. 36 is convenient for turning the screws.

FIG. 36.   Screw Driver.

If the pin of the D key II, which projects a little below, be drawn out, both keys are loosened and can be pushed off the axle. [The translator would advise, unless there is urgent need, that these pins should not be removed. For the purposes of cleaning, it is sufficient to remove the several groups of keys from the body, and to clean these groups without separating them into single pieces.] By unscrewing the small steel axles on which the rollers turn, these may also be removed from the lever arms.

To remove the D♯ key III, unscrew the steel axle and draw it out of the hinge.

By unscrewing the pointed screw *d* the lower section 8 to 15 of group *B* may be taken off, and likewise the upper section 16 to 20 may be removed by unscrewing the upper steel axle which forms the pivot at 20. The keys can be slipped off the moveable steel axles as soon as the pins through the clutch joints are pushed out.

To remove the C key XII, partly draw out the steel axle which goes entirely through the C♯ key XIII.

In the group *C* the two keys G♯ VIII and A IX, in similar fashion, are taken off by withdrawing, partially or wholly, the steel axle which is screwed into the sphere *h*.

For the removal of the two trill keys D XIV and D♯ XV of group *D*, loosen the pointed screw in the spherical pillar *l*. The D key XIV as well as its hinge can be drawn off the steel axle as soon as the pin through the lever arm at 28 (D♯ lever) is pushed out.

When taking off and separating the key mechanism, it is best to lay each separate piece in its proper order on a sheet of paper; this will much facilitate the putting together, and it will not be so easy to interchange or lose anything. Each piece can then be readily cleaned and polished.

All the surfaces may be cleaned with a cloth or chamois skin, and the inside of the hinge tubes with a small feather or a tuft of cotton which may be pushed through the little tubes with a small stick of wood, etc. [or be drawn through with a fine copper wire].

After this cleaning the surfaces may best be polished with a piece of fine glove leather [chamois skin] and a fine polishing brush with the application of a little rouge, such as is used by jewelers.

When putting the mechanism together again, all the places at which rubbing occurs must be properly oiled. For this purpose watch oil is best, but one may also use neats-foot oil or perfectly pure olive oil which has stood in the sun for a time and thereby been purified by sedimentary precipitation.

The steel axles should be wiped with a little piece of cloth slightly wet with oil, and the pointed screws (pivots) are best oiled with the point of a wooden toothpick. One should not use more oil than is really necessary for the protection of the rubbing surfaces.

In putting together and screwing on the mechanism, as is self-evident, one must in each particular follow exactly the reverse order to that which was used in taking the instrument apart. It is necessary in each key group first to joint the pieces, after sliding them over the steel axles, by tightly inserting the pins; the separate groups of keys are screwed on, and finally the springs are hooked.

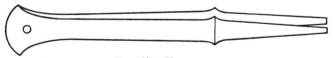

FIG. 37.   Tweezers.

For holding the little screws, pins and springs, tweezers such as are shown in Fig. 37, are useful.

For cementing leather or cloth [or cork] linings which have fallen off the keys, etc., a proper solution of shellac in alcohol serves best.

(c) THE KEY PADS

The most careful attention must be given to the proper construction and adjustment of the key pads. The pads are made from a strong cloth-like stuff of fine wool [felt]. In order that the pads may close the holes air tight, these felt disks are covered with a fine membrane (skin); this membrane is usually doubled, so that any accidental injury to the pad shall not become troublesome all at once.

The pads are covered over on the back side with little sheets of card and a hole is punched through the center, so that they may be screwed fast in the key cups. It is hardly possible to make the key cups always come exactly to the edge of the tone-holes; the pads are therefore made of such thickness that there is left a little space, then by underlaying of card or paper disks this may be filled till the pad fits perfectly all around. The failure of the pad to close the hole at particular points can be remedied by using pieces of paper cut in crescent shape.

The pads are held by screws, the nuts being soldered to the key cups, and under the heads of the little screws there are silver washers, which must be allowed to press the pad neither too tightly nor too lightly; in the first case little wrinkles are formed in the skin of the pad which interfere with the air tight closing, in the second case air may escape through the cup.

If a washer is too loosely held by its screw, it may be set in vibration by certain tones, producing an audible buzz which is inexplicable to many. It has happened that flutes have been sent from distances of several hundred miles for repairs on which there was nothing wrong except that one single screw was not sufficiently tight.

The main point about the pads is that each separate key must close the corresponding hole perfectly air tight; and when one key is required to operate upon another this can be accurately adjusted by means of the regulating screws applied by me.

When one key acts upon another, as the E key upon the G key, one can determine by seeing light between the pad and its seat or by the pressure of the finger whether one key presses too hard or too lightly; the regulating screw must be turned backward or forward until the two keys close together.

In the case of the double connected keys, where the F♯ key works the G key and the B key together, first turn the adjusting screw in the clutch of the F♯ key, and regulate the action of the G key, and then, afterwards adjust the action of the B key.

To prove that all the keys on the middle joint or on the foot joint close perfectly, stop one end with a fine cork, and blow into the other end, while all the keys are closed with the fingers; one can then determine whether or not the air leaks out. By strongly blowing in tobacco smoke it will be easily seen which key leaks. But, a more certain way is to draw out the air, after which the fingers are removed; if then all the keys remain closed of themselves, it is a sure indication no air leaks in.

Fig. 38 is a clamp made of steel wire with which the keys can be pressed upon the flute until the pads become perfectly seated.

FIG. 38.   Clamp for the pads.

Upon removing a pad which is still useful, one should designate its correct position in relation to the key stem by a mark, so that upon replacing it, it will come exactly into its former position.

I have given these explanations so minutely, because the certain speaking and pure quality of tone of a flute depend in a great measure upon a perfect closing of the key, and this again upon a good padding. Well made pads, which I have in stock, can easily be sent in letters as "samples without value."

(d) THE SPRINGS

Of all metals, steel, undoubtedly, is the best for making springs. The genuine English darning or sewing needles of fine cast steel, well hardened, perfectly polished, which can be had in all required lengths and thicknesses, the best fulfill all the requirements of good key springs.

Their preparation is quite simple. When it is necessary to replace a broken spring by a new one, select a needle of the proper length and of exactly the same thickness as the broken one, accurately fitting the hole in the spring post, so that it may be drawn in tight without being drawn through. When a proper needle is found, lay it on a thin piece of sheet iron, and hold it over an alcohol flame long enough for it to become uniformly of a beautiful blue or dark violet color. It thus loses its too great brittleness, and it can be easily bent as much as is necessary for obtaining the required tension, without danger of breaking. The needle may then be notched with a file at the right length and the superfluous end broken off. For this a fine sharp edged file is useful. The bending and inserting of the springs is accomplished by means of small pincers, Fig. 39.

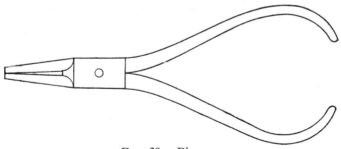

Fig. 39. Pincers.

If steel springs break, it is almost always because of rust, which readily forms in damp air or from the perspiration of the fingers. A sudden breaking of a spring while playing is very disagreeable. To prevent this, I have sometimes made springs of hard-drawn gold wire, which cost only 4 Thalers extra; these are next to steel springs in elasticity, and for many years have proved themselves very durable.

(e) The Cork in the Head Joint

Since the perfect tuning of the octaves depends upon the proper closing of the air column by the cork, it is necessary to smear it well with tallow each time it is drawn out for wiping the head joint.

If the cork fits too tightly, it can be made a little smaller by rolling between two smooth surfaces such as a table top and small board. Conversely the cork may be made shorter and consequently thicker by means of a cabinet maker's screw clamp.

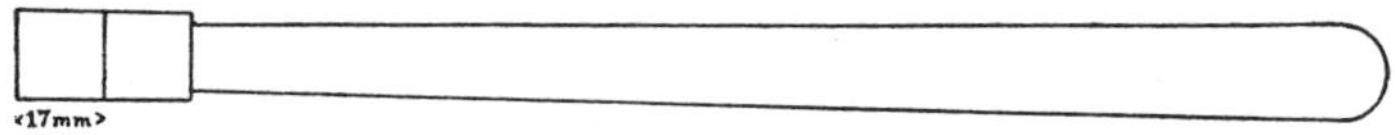

‹17mm›

Fig. 40. Gauge for setting the cork.

That one may always place the cork exactly at the correct distance of 17 millimeters [about $\frac{11}{16}$ inch] from the center of the mouth-hole, it is best to have a mark on the projecting end of the cork screw, and for verification to have also an accurate measuring stick such as is shown in Fig. 40.

THEOBALD BOEHM

Aged 33 years

From a miniature painted on ivory by Brandmüller

IX. TREATMENT OF THE FLUTE IN GENERAL

IN order that a flute may remain in good condition as long as possible, it must be handled with care and cleanliness. Generally one has only himself to blame for the larger repairs required, for cracks in the wood or breaks in the mechanism are usually the result of carelessness and neglect of cleanliness. Such accidents are easily prevented. If the cork coverings of both joints of the middle part of a wood flute are well rubbed with pure tallow, they will then remain soft and will tightly close the joints against moisture; and the application of undue force when putting the parts together will become unnecessary. For the same reason, the draw tube of the head joint, and the socket tube on the lower end of the middle joint of a silver flute must always be covered with tallow.

To avoid injury to the key mechanism, the middle joint should always be grasped by the upper end, and never in the middle; and similarly the foot-joint should be grasped with the hand on the lower end.

The three pieces should be so put together that the flute may be held in a natural position. The mouth-hole, the centers of the upper holes on the middle joint, and the axles of the foot keys should coincide in one straight line. The crutch should

be inserted and so turned that the weight of the
flute rests between the thumb and index finger
of the left hand, then the movements of the fingers will be much freer than when the thumb is
used for holding the flute. [The crutch is shown at
C in Figs. 27 and 28, and also in Fig. 33.]

[The translator agrees with Rockstro, who, in
his "Treatise on the Flute," says: "The crutch
is a cumbersome and unsightly appendage, and
is useless to those who have properly constructed
flutes, and who know how to hold them. It seriously cramps the action of the left hand fingers,
especially the thumb, while it is unproductive of
a single advantage. Happily it is now almost
obsolete."]

Further, one should be certain that the flute
is so held in the hand that no water can flow
into the tone-holes, since pads covered with moisture easily stick to the edges of the holes.

When the flute is laid down out of the hand,
the crutch should be turned at right angles to the
flute tube so that it will form a firm support for
the flute as it rests upon a horizontal plane, the
flute tube itself inclining downwards.

If a pad should become accidentally wet and for
this reason or because of dirt, should stick, push
a strip of printing paper under the pad and again
draw it out while gently pressing down on the key.
In this way the moisture and dirt will be rubbed
off the smooth skin of the pad, and will adhere
to the rough surface of the paper.

If one takes the further slight trouble, each

time the flute is laid down, to wipe the perspiration of the fingers from the keys, the oxidation of the metal will be retarded, and the flute will remain clean and bright for a long time.

The most important matter in the care of flutes, especially of new wooden ones, is the wiping out of the tube. The warping out of shape of the wood, which alters the proportions of the bore, and causes most of the cracks, is the result of moisture, which collects in the flute tube during the blowing. This produces an unequal expansion, the consequence of which is often the formation of superficial ridges, and frequently the complete bursting of the wood.

Consequently after each blowing the flute tube must be wiped perfectly clean and dry, for which purpose one had best use an old silk or fine linen handkerchief and a thin swab stick of the length of the middle joint. Fold one end of the corner of the cloth over the stick and push it through the flute, till the upper end can be taken hold of. Then by slowly drawing the cloth through, all the drops of the liquid will be taken up by the first part of the cloth while the following part which is yet dry will completely remove any remaining moisture.

Upon repeating this operation many times the bore will become polished, facilitating the full and easy production of tone; and this also makes it entirely superfluous to oil the flute tube, which is both disagreeable and injurious to the pads.

X. ON THE BLOWING OF NEW FLUTES

EXPERIENCE shows that all wood-wind instruments are affected by the manner of blowing so that they become either better or worse with regard to the tones and their production. Though the tuning proportions remain unaltered, yet the player can accustom himself to blow single tones higher or lower.

The reasons for this have never yet been satisfactorily explained. But it is known, that even after all swellings and deformations of the wood are removed from the flute tube as much as possible by the most careful swabbings, the influence of the manner of blowing still remains perceptible. The best flute loses an easy speech by overblowing and its bright clear quality of tone by a bad embouchure, and conversely gains in speech and tone by a correct handling and a good embouchure.

The formation of a good embouchure is therefore not only of the utmost importance for flute playing in general, but especially for the blowing of new flutes. Consequently a knowledge of the origin of the tone will be helpful.

THEOBALD BOEHM

Aged 35 years

At the time of the development of the conical bore, ring-key, flute

XI. THE EMBOUCHURE

THE column of air enclosed by the tube of the flute is exactly comparable with a stretched violin string. As the string is set into transverse vibrations by the bow and thus is made to sound, so the longitudinal vibrations of the air column of the flute are produced by the blowing.

Further, as the clear quality of tone of the violin depends upon a proper manipulation of the bow, so also the pure flute tone depends upon the direction in which the air stream is blown against the edge of the mouth-hole.

Depending upon whether the air stream is directed more or less below the horizontal as it is blown across the flute, there develops from the fundamental tone of the flute tube, with all the holes closed, the so-called aliquot or harmonic overtones; e. g., for the fundamental tone C_3, the aliquot tones are C_4, G_4, C_5, E_5, G_5, (B_5b), and C_6.

Each octave therefore requires a different direction of the air stream, and when the correct one is found, not merely will a fine quality of tone be brought out, but by increasing the force of the air blast, the tone may be brought to the greatest possible strength without any deterioration in quality or pitch.

However, by overblowing, that is by violently

forcing the air, any tone can be made to break
over into the higher tones, even when only a portion of the air goes in the right direction. Not
only through the air thus wasted, but also because
of the poor embouchure, the tone loses in purity,
and there is produced at the same time a buzzing
and rushing noise.

XII. THE BASS FLUTE IN G

(a) Its Musical Characteristics

IN closing [in the original this section appeared at the end of the "Conclusion"] I feel that I ought to mention one of the most recently perfected, and therefore little known, developments of the flute, to the construction of which I was led by the great facility of vibration and easy speech of my silver flute in C; I refer to the "Alt-Flöte" in G [Bass Flute] which is pitched a major fourth below the flute in C.

The long felt need for deeper, stronger, and at the same time more sonorous flute tones has not been satisfactorily provided for either by the former "Flûte d'amour" or by the extension to the foot of a C flute, since the tones thus obtained are weak and uncertain, and their combination difficult and entirely unpracticable. There must be created an entirely new instrument in the family of flutes of deeper pitch, similar to the basset-horn and the English horn.

[The exact date of the origin of the bass flute is uncertain. The booklet, "Zur Erinnerung an Theobald Boehm," states: "In his sixtieth year Boehm made his Alt-Flöte which produces a remarkable effect." This would make the year 1854 or 1855. In several letters dated in 1865, Boehm refers to the flute in G as being well established.]

[Fig. 41 shows a bass flute in G made by Boehm and Mendler, acording to their most approved design. Fig. 42 is an instrument of the same kind with slight improvements in the mechanism, made by Rudall, Carte and Company.]

Because of the great facility for modulation of the full, sonorous tones of this flute, it is adapted to music in the song style, and for accompanying a soprano voice. A player will, after a very little practice, be in a position to bring out *genre* effects which are impossible upon the C flute.

[Flutists have sometimes misunderstood the purpose of the flute in G, thinking it ought to be like the flute in C in quality but lower in pitch. It was Boehm's purpose to produce "an entirely new instrument," with a quality distinctly different from that of the flute in C even when tones of the same pitch were sounded on both flutes. The difference is similar to that between a true soprano voice and a true contralto. The quality of the lower register of the flute in G sometimes mildly suggests tones of the same pitch of the violin, or the French horn, or the saxophone played softly.]

[Flutes of low pitch have long been made by many makers, often descending a full octave below middle C, as in the so-called contra-bass flutes. An account of flutes of lower pitch is given in Chapter VIII of Fitzgibbon's "Story of the Flute," reprinted in the *Flutist* magazine for November, 1920, page 244. Boehm's distinct contribution was in so proportioning the tube as to secure the

Fig. 41.
Bass Flute
Boehm & Mendler

Fig. 42.
Bass Flute
Rudall, Carte & Co.

desired characteristic tone-quality, and in so ar-
ranging the key mechanism that the fingering remains the same as for the Flute in C, and so that
the operation is as certain and easy.   The flute
in G plays very easily, with an embouchure a little more relaxed than for the flute in C, and with
gentler blowing; the mechanism is so reliable
that the execution is just as clear and certain as
for the flute in C, though on account of the larger
size of the keys, it is not suitable for very rapid
passages.   Its effective compass is about two and
a half octaves.   A Flute in F becomes so long
that the mechanism is less satisfactory in operation.   On the other hand the Alto Flute in B♭ is
as playable as the flute in C, and is intermediate
between this and the flute in G as regards tone
quality.]

[In a letter to Mr. Broadwood dated August,
1871, (Broadwood, "Essay," page 59), Boehm
writes: "My ideal of tone, large, sonorous, and
powerful, admitting of every gradation from
pianissimo to *fortissimo,* is still the tone of my
silver flute in G.   The effect I have repeatedly
produced, when playing it, although now I am an
old man of 78½ years, is such that I only regret
that I did not make this flute forty years ago.
With a silver head-joint and a gold embouchure,
the tone is very brilliant, and no room is too large
for it; while with a wood embouchure on the silver head-joint, the tone gains in richness without
losing in power.   Once when I played in church
on this flute, accompanying a soprano, it was mis-

taken for a French horn." In another letter dated
February, 1873, he writes: "My eightieth birth-
day will be in a few weeks, nevertheless I play
every morning on my flute in G and people like to
hear it." The translator has used a flute in G for
over twenty years, and very much prefers it to the
flute in C for music in the song style.]

[Notwithstanding its beautiful tone quality the
flute in G has been used but little. However,
modern orchestral composers are now scoring for
it, parts being found in the following compositions: Ravel, *Daphnis et Chloe;* Weingarten, *Die
Gefilde der Seligen;* Mahler, *Symphonies;* Hol-
brooke, *Children of Don* and *Dylan;* Stanford, various compositions; Hahn, *A Ballet;* Schmid, *Joseph
and His Brethren;* Stravinsky, *Le Sacre du Prin-
temps;* Rimsky-Karsakow, *Ballet Mlada,* and *Ivan
the Terrible;* Glazunow, various compositions;
Atterberg, *Ocean Symphony.*]

[The flute in G is particularly suited to chamber music, solos, duets, trios, etc., and yet very
little music has ever been published for it. Rudall,
Carte and Company, of London, have issued the
following pieces for the flute in G and piano:
Beethoven, *Adelaide;* Mendelssohn, *Elijah, If With
All Your Hearts* and *O, Rest in the Lord;* Mozart,
Aria, *Il mio tesoro,* and *Andante* (arranged by
Boehm); Schubert, *Serenade.* Boehm arranged
a number of pieces but these have remained in
manuscript with the single exception noted above;
a list of these arrangements is given in the appendix, and probably any flutist can himself re-

arrange them from other available scores. Violin music of the song style is especially suitable, as the flute in G begins on the same tone as the G string of the violin. The part for the violin may be easily transposed. The following pieces have been found very effective: Bach, *Air for the G String* (Wilhelmj); Godard, *Adagio Pathétique;* Schumann, *Träumerei* and *Abendgebet;* Godard, *Berceuse from Jocelyn;* Terschak, *Romance Italienne.* Many trios for Flute, Violin, and Piano are beautifully rendered when the Flute in G takes the violin part; an effective number of this kind is the *Romanza* by Fuchs.]

(b) DIMENSIONS OF THE BASS FLUTE

As early as 1847 I had made flute tubes giving an easy and certain speech for the tone E_2

but the difficulties connected with the construction and playing of the keys led me to choose the tone G_2

as the fundamental of my bass flute.

In the calculation of the proportions of the air column, I gave preference to the deeper tones; the speech is easy and certain, and lends itself to a surprisingly strong *crescendo;* hence the bass flute is suitable for playing in the largest room or in the *salon.*

[Boehm submitted a flute in G, together with an explanation of his *Schema*, to the Paris Exposition of 1867, and as a part of the exhibit there were tables of the actual dimensions of his flutes in C and G. The table for the flute in C is given on page 35 of this work; the table for the Flute in G was not included by Boehm in "Die Flöte und das Flötenspiel," but for the sake of completeness and because of increasing interest, it seems desirable to include it in this edition. Comments on the exhibit at the Paris Exhibition are given on pages 309 to 313 of Welch's "History of the Boehm Flute."]

[As made by Boehm the flute in G has a tube with an inside diameter of 26 millimeters; the tone-holes are 19.3 millimeters in diameter and the rise of the keys is about 6 millimeters; the embouchure is a trifle larger than for the flute in C, being about 11.0 by 13.0 millimeters; the distance of the face of the cork from the center of the embouchure is 20.5 millimeters; Table III gives the scale for such a flute corresponding to the pitch A=435. From these dimensions a *Schema* diagram for the flute in G at various pitches can be constructed in the manner described for the flute in C, on pages 35 to 47. The "actual length of air column" for any tone is the distance, measured from the face of the cork to the center of the corresponding lateral tone-hole having a diameter of 19.3 millimeters. This length is 68 millimeters less than the corresponding "theoretical length"; the quantity, 68 millimeters, is the "closed-end correction" for this size of tube (see pages 34 and 42).]

TABLE III

Tones	Absolute Vibration Numbers	Theoretical Lengths of Air Column	Actual Lengths of Air Column
G_3	387.54	442.50mm	374.50mm
G_3b F_3#	365.79	468.81	400.81
F_3	345.26	496.68	428.68
E_3	325.88	526.22	458.22
E_3b D_3#	307.59	557.51	489.51
D_3	290.33	590.66	522.66
D_3b C_3#	274.03	625.78	557.78
C_3	258.65	663.00	595.00
B_2	244.14	702.42	634.42
B_2b A_2#	230.43	733.19	676.19
A_2	217.50	788.44	720.44
A_2b G_2#	205.29	835.32	767.32
G_2	193.77	885.00	817.00

[Other practical details of the dimensions, for the pitch A=435, are as follows: The "correction for the open end" is 10.5 millimeters, so that the distance from the cork, to the end giving the lowest tone, G_2, is 817+10.5=827.5 millimeters. The correction for the F# hole is − 2.3 millimeters, giving for the actual location of this hole, 557.8 − 2.3= 555.5 millimeters from the cork. The C# hole is 10 millimeters in diameter and it is at a distance of 333.0 millimeters from the cork. The D♮ trill-key hole has a diameter of 10.5 millimeters and it is 315.2 millimeters from the cork. The octave-key hole is 5.0 millimeters in diameter and is 13.9 millimeters above the C# hole.]

[The bass flute shown in Fig. 41 is constructed according to the *Schema* based upon the dimensions of Table III, and is for the pitch A=440.]

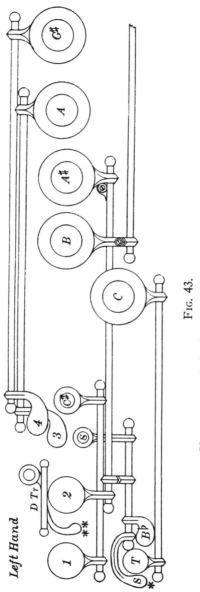

FIG. 43.

Upper part of the key mechanism of the Bass Flute.

(c) Mechanism of the Bass Flute

Being made with G for its fundamental tone, there is required no alteration in the system of fingering, since the upper half of the key mechanism can be arranged to be played very conveniently by the left hand, through extensions of the axles, as shown in Fig. 43, and the lower half requires only slight alterations.

A very conveniently arranged "schleifklappe" [octave-key], marked S and with a * in Fig. 43, may be opened by the thumb; it serves to give freer speech and greater purity of tone to the notes $D_4{}^\sharp$, $E_4\flat$, D_5, $D_5{}^\sharp$, $E_5\flat$ and A_5. [This key is described and illustrated, as applied to the flute in C, on page 86.]

The trill key, marked D and * * in Fig. 43, is a substitute for the long D trill key in all cases where this would be used on the C flute.

[The mechanism of the flute shown in Fig. 41 is arranged exactly as shown in the diagram Fig. 43, and explained in the preceding paragraphs. The mechanism of the flute shown in Fig. 42 is the same in general, except that there are trill keys for D and D♯, to be played by the fingers of the right hand as on the ordinary C flute, and there is no octave-key. This construction for the trill keys is the one now usually employed.]

(d) Special Fingerings for the Bass Flute

All the fingerings of the C flute from C_3 to A_5 are applicable to the bass flute; but since the C_3 sounds as G_2, of course the music for the bass flute

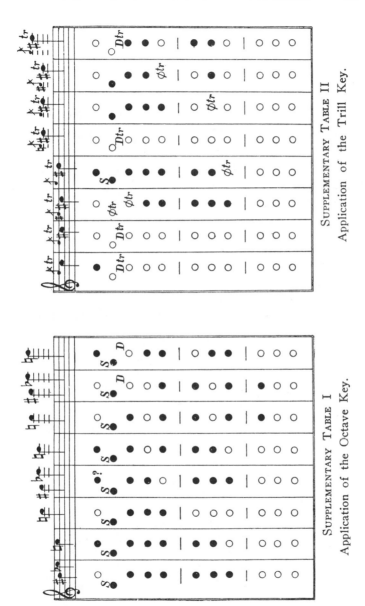

SUPPLEMENTARY TABLE II
Application of the Trill Key.

SUPPLEMENTARY TABLE I
Application of the Octave Key.

must be written a fourth higher, that is, be transposed. [The tables of regular fingerings for the C flute are given on page 72.]

On p. 129 are two supplementary tables of fingerings; the first shows the application of the octave-key *, Fig. 43; the second table indicates the special uses of the D trill key, * *, Fig. 43. [As mentioned above, the bass flute is usually constructed with trill keys placed as on the C flute, in which case the fingerings for the latter are directly applicable.]

THEOBALD BOEHM

Aged 60 years

At the time of the perfection of the cylinder bore, covered hole, flute

His favorite portrait

PART II

FLUTE-PLAYING

PART II—FLUTE-PLAYING

XIII. THE DEVELOPMENT OF TONE

UPON the supposition that the student has had elementary musical instruction in regard to notes, time, keys, etc., such as may be found in any printed Flute Instructor (especially in that of Hugot and Wunderlich, Jos. Aibl, Munich) I will proceed to a consideration of the playing of the flute itself, and shall begin with what I believe to be the essential requisite, the tone formation.

A good embouchure depends for the most part upon a normal formation of the lips and teeth. However, if one has a defective embouchure, and also lacks a proper appreciation of beautiful tone quality, that is if he does not have a proper tone sense, both of these faults can be considerably improved by exercising in the following manner.

Since a gradual transition is best in all things, by passing from the easy to the more difficult, so one, in blowing a new flute, should not begin with the higher and lower tones which are more difficult to produce, but he should begin in the middle register, in which the tone C_4 is best produced by a beginner. [This tone is produced when the first finger of the left hand only is placed on its key.]

When one has found the proper embouchure by which this tone can be clearly sounded in a delicate *piano,* one should gradually, without raising the pitch, swell it to a *forte,* and then bring it back again to the faintest *pianissimo.*

When this is fully accomplished one passes in the following manner to the next lower tone. While sounding the C₄ with a beautiful, clear, and pure tone, close the C key by a quick motion [of the left thumb], but without making any alteration in the embouchure or in the force of the wind.

The tone B thus obtained should continue, un-altered, the quality and purity of the preceding tone C. Then sound the B alone [with *crescendo*

and *diminuendo*], and after breathing again, pro-ceed [in like manner] to the tone B♭.

Continuing in this way and with the least pos-sible alteration of the embouchure, gradually, cer-tainly and without exertion proceed to the lower tones successively, and in a similar manner prac-tice the tones from C₄ upwards to the highest. Since each tone is always developed out of the preceding tone, which is already as perfect as possible, all of the tones will remain equally perfect in quality, strength and purity.

As soon as one obtains a certainty in the embouchure, he should next practice all the major and minor scales; then intervals of thirds, fourths, fifths, sixths, sevenths, and octaves; the embouchure will thus become accustomed to the making of increasing intervals, and soon one will be in a position to take the greatest skips with the proper embouchure, and consequently with certainty.

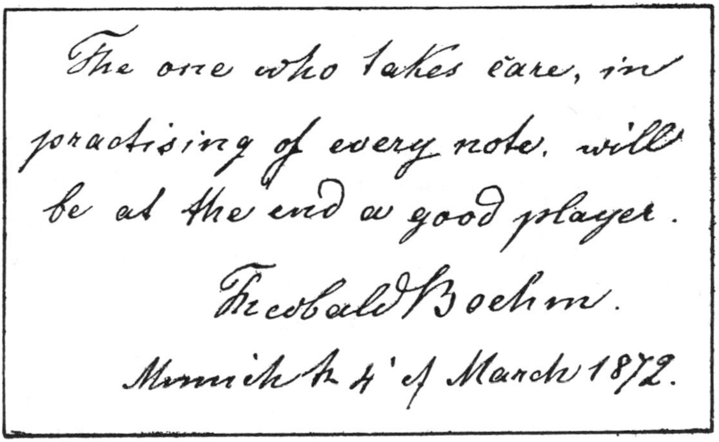
The one who takes care, in practising of every note, will be at the end a good player.
Theobald Boehm.
Munich th 4' of March 1872.

FIG. 44.
Facsimile of Boehm's autograph.

XIV. FINGER EXERCISES

SINCE the certain production of the tone depends not only upon the embouchure, but also upon a quick and smooth movement of the fingers, in this exercise all the tones should be slurred together, for in staccato playing one observes less easily whether all the fingers move up and down precisely together.

A portion of one's attention is always lost in reading notes, therefore, it is very important to play "by heart" as much as possible, so that the formation of the embouchure and tone may have the undivided attention. To do this will, of course, be difficult for the untrained musician. The best method for impressing upon the memory the proper sequence of tones in the scales and chords of all keys, is first to learn by heart the tones of one scale or one chord in only a single octave; then one will soon learn to play the flute in all keys and through its entire compass. Furthermore I have come to the conclusion from my own practice as well as from my many years of experience as a teacher, that pupils advance most rapidly who take the trouble to practice patiently the complicated finger changes of a single difficult phrase until it can be played smoothly and clearly. One acquires in this way, so to speak, wealth which is laid by, and which is always increasing by additions.

When a short phrase is found difficult, it is evidently a waste of time to repeat the entire passage containing the "stumbling block" in the greater part of which one has already acquired facility; one should practice the few troublesome notes till the difficult tone-combination is mastered.

By such a judicious use of time I have brought many scholars in a year's practice to a thoroughly correct interpretation (execution) of a piece of music which others with far greater talent, but without patience and perseverance, would never acquire.

An answer is needed to the question which is so frequently put to me, "What and how should one first practice in learning my flute?" Notwithstanding this work makes no claim to the title of a Flute-School, yet this is an appropriate place for the answer and the many interested flute players will welcome it.

XV. THE METHOD OF PRACTICING

ABOVE all one should endeavor, at the beginning of each practice period, to secure a good embouchure, in the manner previously described, for without a clear tone, nothing can be well and beautifully played. The tone is the voice without which one cannot even begin to sing.

When the embouchure has become good and certain, one should study the scales and chords in all the keys, for these are the foundation of all passages, and when one has once learned to play them with precise finger movements (which can be easily determined by the ear) all the other tone figures will be quickly and easily mastered.

As has been said, it is only a waste of time to repeat anything that can already be played without stumbling. Difficult finger movements, on the contrary, must be gone over very slowly at first, so that in the slurred tone-combinations no interpolated tones are audible, and no lack of purity is noticeable. Especially, one must train the fingers to a perfectly smooth movement by the trill exercises, so that no one tone predominates, and so that no bleating or so-called "bockstriller" [goat trill] is produced.

To secure this smoothness, there must be no perceptible cramping tension of the muscles, in either the hand or arm; this cramping results from an entirely unnecessary expenditure of force.

If one only forms the idea that a thing is not difficult, it becomes much easier.

Further, many flute players have the bad habit of raising the fingers not only much too high, but also to unequal heights, whereby complicated finger movements become unnecessarily difficult; since when several keys are closed at the same time, if one finger must move much farther than another, it is perfectly evident that they cannot reach the end at the same time.

The raising of the fingers too high has another disadvantage, since in rapidly closing the keys a very audible and disagreeable clap or rattle is produced, and at the same time the key receives a blow and the mechanism a reaction which clearly work disadvantageously to them. On the contrary, if the fingers are held directly over the keys a forcible closing of them will be nearly or wholly inaudible, and there will be produced only a pressure without rebound.

The fingers therefore should be held at equal heights, and no higher than is necessary above the keys. To secure this, and especially as most players do not realize how high they have raised their fingers, I advise all my pupils, when practicing the scales, to stand before a mirror. They are then in a position to see not only the finger movements and the whole manner of holding the flute, but also to detect many bad habits, such as distortion of the features, and unnecessary movements of the head, arms and body.

If one cannot express his feelings through the style of tone, he surely is not in a position to do so by head or body movements. A calm, firm attitude certainly presents a much more pleasing appearance to the hearer than visible exertions, or affected, sentimental movements.

Since bad habits are very difficult to overcome, they ought to be removed in their beginnings. It is very short sighted to economize in the beginning, for in the end the best teacher is also the cheapest. It is impossible for everyone to find a good teacher, and in all the flute-schools known to me the methods of style are treated in a very superficial manner; therefore, I believe that my views upon this subject, founded upon many years of experience as an artist and teacher, should be given.

ANTOINE SACCHETTI AND THEOBALD BOEHM

XVI. MUSICAL INTERPRETATION

HE who, like myself, has been fortunate enough to have heard, for more than fifty years, all the greatest singers and songstresses of the time, will never forget the names of Brizzi, Sesi, Catalani, Velluti, Lablache, Tamburini, Rubini, Malibran, Pasta, etc. It fills me with joy to remember their artistic and splendid performances; they have all come forth from the good old Italian school of song, which today, as in the past hundred years, gives the foundation for a good voice formation, and leads to a correct understanding of style, which is an essential for the instrumentalist as well as for the singer.

The interpretation of a piece of music should evidently give to the hearer what the composer has endeavored to express in notes. The player himself must therefore, in order to be intelligible, first clearly comprehend the sense and spirit of the composition.

But the means which the composer has at hand are not always sufficient to clearly convey his ideas. All the customary designations of the tempo from *largo* to *prestissimo* being without metronomic determinations give rather indefinite ideas; and the articulations, accents, and nuances of the tone strength, especially in older or carelessly copied music, are designated at the best in a very faulty way and often not at all. Much is left therefore to the discretion and individual comprehension of the performer, in which respects, as is known, even thorough musicians will differ considerably.

In the orchestra, naturally the interpretation of the director is followed and the flutist who plays each note according to the dictated directions, clearly, with a good and pure tone, has accomplished much, and his playing is at least correct.

In solo playing, on the other hand, where the player himself appears, the overcoming of technical difficulties is mainly accomplished by an extraordinary amount of practice, after which the genuine artist should endeavor to bring out a definite expression of feeling. It is much easier to win applause by a brilliant execution, than to reach the hearts of the hearers through a *cantabile*.

For example, to play well an *adagio* with all the possible colorature, the player must not only be a perfect master of his instrument, but he must also have the power to transform the tones, as it were, into words, by which he will be able to give his feelings a clear expression. The composer of vocal music endeavors to make the tones express the emotions described by the words, and the singer is most easily led to a correct musical interpretation through the words connected with the tones; likewise, the flute player must learn to sing upon his instrument.

If the composer under the influence of the words

of the poem has been enabled to express his feelings in tone, and to form his melodies upon the laws of rhythm and declamation, so also the thoughtful instrumentalist can perceive the correct interpretation of the music of an aria or a song in its text.

He will learn by the study of good song music when and why a note should be played staccato, or be slurred with the next following; and when an accent or a crescendo or diminuendo in the tone strength, is necessary to bestow upon the music an expression corresponding to the words; and when a breath can be taken without breaking the correct declamation.

The text will clearly show him the phrases and will indicate to him the points for which the full strength of the tone must be saved, for producing the greatest effects, as is done by the points of highest light in a good painting.

The following examples will serve as a clearer explanation of what has been said, as well as to explain the *portamento di voce* which is indispensable to a good style of cantabile.

Since it is only possible to indicate the declamation or correct expression of the words of a text on an instrument by means of articulation, that is by striking the notes according to the meaning or syllable-beginnings of the words, it is important to learn the necesary art of tonguing and its proper application. This is indicated in three different ways, namely a short staccato by little lines

($\dot{\complement}\dot{\complement}\dot{\complement}$)   ; less staccato by points   ($\dot{\complement}\dot{\complement}\dot{\complement}$)

and an entirely smooth staccato by points over

which there is a slur   ($\overset{\frown}{\dot{\complement}\dot{\complement}\dot{\complement}}$) , indicating that

the tone is to have merely a new impulse, but that the air stream is not to be interrupted.

This tonguing should sound as softly as the second syllable "de" [*tē*] for example, in speaking the word "Beide" [*bī-tē*], which serves very satisfactorily for the making of separate syllables. In many cases the expression can be further increased, as is indicated in the following example.

[The musical illustrations have been photographically reproduced from the German edition. The line above the words is the music as written for the voice, while the line below indicates the interpretation for the flute.]

The correct articulation follows here of itself from the declamation of the words.

By means of the soft tonguing of the four notes
Eb, D, C, and Bb of the first bar, as well as the notes
D, C, Bb and Ab of the third bar, there is given
to the words "ist bezaubernd schön," and "kein
Auge je gesehn," considerably more expression
than if they were entirely slurred together. The
breathing places are indicated thus: v.

Further, it is evident that it is not allowable to
slur any note over to the first note of the next
measure, since it almost always happens that the
note falling in the so-called strong part of the
measure must be tongued, in order that the word
depending upon it may receive its proper accent.
The slurring of a note to the following measure
is always a fault, unless it is justified for some
special reason, as in dance music or comic songs,
where it may be used to produce a piquant or
bizarre effect. For example:

But in song music this tying over from the
weak to the strong beat of a measure is allowable
only when employed as syncopation, as in canon
or fugue, to bring out an increased expression. For
example in the following illustration where the

word "nur" is repeated in the third measure, the anticipation of the E by a quarter note constitutes a syncopation, by means of which the effect is increased.

The following examples will furnish, through a reading of the text, a clear idea of the rhythmic and declamatory significance of each note.

The methods of interpretation which I have here given for playing on the flute, will serve as guides by which anyone may learn to judge correctly why and in what manner a note should be tongued or intoned, so that it shall give the sense and expression of the word for which it is a substitute, or whether it should be considered merely as a syllable without significance, and should therefore be slurred together with other notes.

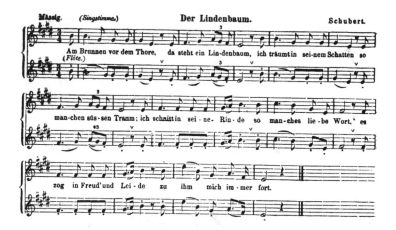

Upon the repetition of a strophe, on the contrary, where the theme would become somewhat monotonous in the absence of words, the player may be allowed to take some license, and add little ornaments in suitable places; especially in bright and light melodies. In the last of the following songs, "Das Fischermädchen," for example, a heightening of the expression will result, if the ornaments are performed not heavily, but lightly and gracefully.

In the preceding song the triplets, and also the sixteenth notes of the second, fourth and sixth measures of the following, may be slurred; however, in my opinion, a soft tonguing gives a more definite effect.

The triplets may also be slurred together, in the above song.

The great wealth of beautiful German songs of Mozart, Beethoven, Schubert, Mendelssohn and others are almost inexhaustible sources of studies for the formation of a correct interpretation and a good style.

From the words of the poems of the popular songs of other nations, such as Scottish, Irish, Swedish and Slavish, one may also learn a good interpretation.

One should begin with songs which are simple but full of expression in word and melody, then one will soon learn to comprehend compositions, which, as Beethoven's "Adelaide," are written in the highest dramatic style, and form a transition to the arias for the interpretation of which a knowledge of all the arts of ornamentation and colorature is necessary.

All coloratures may be considered a diversification of a single note, whose time value is partially or wholly consumed in executing the ornaments.

The simplest ornament is the accented appoggiatura which moves either upwards or downwards, and is designated by a small note; and for equally divided notes it takes one-half of the time value of the principal note, and for unequal division it takes one-third.

[The musical ornaments are first given "as written," and then "as played;" in some instances the name or interpretation seems to be incorrect.]

The double appoggiatura, consisting of two or three small notes, is to be treated in a similar manner. This may form a triplet, as in the examples:

The double appoggiatura is to be distinguished from the "schneller" or half-mordent in which the first of the two small notes is always the same as the principal note; for example:

The true mordent (gruppetto) is a group of three or four small notes which move within the compass of a minor third, and consists, both in ascending and descending, of a note first above and then below the given note. For example:

A very effective, and at the same time the most difficult vocal ornament is the trill, a thoroughly good execution of which is, at the present time, unfortunately, very rarely heard. The trill consists in the alternation of two adjacent tones, a major or a minor second part, which are to be smoothly and rapidly repeated. Following the best old Italian school of song, the trill should commence upon the principal note, and not upon the auxiliary note; the two notes must have equal tone strength, and exactly equal time value, and the alternation should be slower in Adagio, and more rapid in Allegro. For a final cadence, or a fermata, it should gradually increase in speed, and there should be a swelling out and a diminishing of the tone strength. Further, every trill must end with a resolution which is formed of the principal note preceded by the next lower note. The "Pralltriller" [inverted mordent] is the only exception to this rule. For a cadence trill the ending may have a variety of forms, according to the taste of the performer.

Cadence trill.

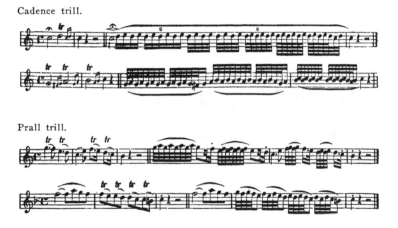

Prall trill.

According to my idea, all trills not resting upon the note of the harmony, such as the last preceding

mordent trills, and trills consisting in the multiplication of an appoggiatura, should begin with

the auxiliary note, and proceed by means of a
final resolution.

All trills must begin slowly, and very gradually
become more rapid, a perfect equality of the tones
being maintained throughout, and the production
of a so-called bleating or "bockstriller" must be
avoided.

Equally useful are the ornaments produced by
runs, which are also developed by the diversification of a fundamental tone and which must therefore be played exactly within the time and in the
manner of expression of this note; either with
equal tone value (*tenuto*) or with increasing
strength (*crescendo*) or diminishing strength
(*diminuendo*). For example:

Since the time of Mozart, and especially by Rossini, all the vocal ornaments have been accurately
written out by composers, hence one will find in
operas and concert arias a large selection of taste-
ful and effective coloratures, which will serve as
models for practice.

Many arias also contain the most beautiful melodies for the study of cantabile which in æsthetic
respects will remain the best examples, and for
the rendering of which the flute player must have

all the qualifications which characterize the genuine artist. These qualifications are an intelligent comprehension of the composition, a deep feeling and a cultivated taste, correctly timed breathing, and a perfectly formed tone, for without these a good interpretation of a cantabile with *portamento* (gliding voice) is impossible.

Although the proper *portamento di voce,* namely the gliding over from one tone to another while speaking two different syllables, is adapted to the human voice alone, and consequently seldom seems good and appropriate on string instruments, yet it is sometimes desired to imitate it upon wind instruments with tone holes. On account of defective execution, however, the effect is often repulsive and suggests "cat music" on the house tops, rather than a beautifully sung *cantilena.*

The significance, often misunderstood, of the word *portamento,* seems to me to consist in a development of the legato derived from the Italian *cantare legato* in which all the intermediate tones are delicately and smoothly connected together, like a series of pearls by a connecting thread, the latter being figuratively represented by the air stream. For example:

The following extract from the aria of Donna Anna in Mozart's "Don Juan" serves as a combination of the above described song-studies, since the cantibile of the Larghetto ends with simple runs and mordent ornaments, and the Allegretto contains mordent trills, roulades, and a closing trill, and has practically all of the arts of colorature.

In the lower line, designed to be played upon the flute, all of the legato places are designated by slur marks, the moderate articulations by points and the sharply tongued notes by lines. The places where breath should be taken are designated by large breathing signs, and the places where it may be taken if necessary by small signs. [In the original edition there are no staccatissimo lines, and the breathing signs are all alike.] The explanation of the trills which occur has already been given above.

FIG. 45.

A photographic reproduction of No. 1 of the 12 Uebungen, in Boehm's own hand-writing.

XVII. CONCLUSION

I BELIEVE that I have now pointed out the surest way in which one may acquire a correct and elegant style of playing, so that he may be prepared to delight himself and others not only with difficult compositions, but also with simple and beautifully played songs.

Moreover, attention to my instructions will lead to a correct technical execution, and to facilitate this there has been printed as a supplement to this work and published by Jos. Aibl in Munich, "12 Uebungsstücke in allen Tonarten." These practice pieces form a transition to the following studies which were composed earlier and in which are to be found nearly all the practicable difficulties for the flute.

1. 12 Etudes pour la Flûte, propres a égaliser le doigté dans toutes les gammes, op. 15; Falter & Sohn, Munich; [Rudall, Carte & Co., London; Carl Fischer, New York.]

2. 24 Caprices-Etudes pour la Flûte, op. 26; B. Schott's Söhne, Mainz; Richault, Paris; Rudall, Carte & Co., London; [Carl Fischer, New York.]

3. 24 Etudes pour la Flûte seule ou avec accompagnement du Piano, op. 37; B. Schott's Söhne, Mainz; [Rudall, Carte & Co., London; Carl Fischer, New York.]

[The original manuscript of this work, mentioned in the Preface, contains the first six of the *Uebungsstücke*. No. 1 of the series is photographically reproduced in Fig. 45, and shows the neatness of Boehm's musical hand-writing. These studies are published by the G. Schirmer Company, New York, in the "Library of Musical Classics," Vol. 122, under the title: "Twelve Practice Pieces for Flute for acquiring a smooth and even finger-movement in all keys."]

[Boehm was not only a famous teacher and a member of the Bavarian Royal Court Orchestra, but he was also widely known for his solo playing in concerts. He frequently appeared in many of the principal music centers of Germany, Hungary, Austria, Italy, Switzerland, France, and England, and the printed accounts of his performances are most complimentary. They show that Boehm himself achieved in a remarkable degree the style of playing which he advocates in this treatise. A published account of one of his concerts in Nuremberg contains the following appreciation: "His playing shows a tender, elegiac sentiment, a beautiful, romantic longing; his singing upon his instrument is inspired by the deepest feeling. His mastership in seizing all *nuances,* the melancholy pathos of his style, wins him the first place among the flutists of Europe. One hesitates to breathe for fear the tenderness and soulfulness of the blended tones will be disturbed and the magic spell will be broken." Of a concert given in Leipzig it is written: "The playing of Herr Boehm is firm, especially pure and technically efficient, with a beautiful, tender, and yet very full tone. The very difficult task in Drouet's 'Variations' he gave with so much finish and good taste that we owe the artist our thanks for an evening full of enjoyment."]

[Boehm wrote over sixty compositions for the flute, including original pieces in various styles and arrangements of the classics, with both piano and orchestral accompaniments. A complete, revised list of Boehm's published compositions is given in the Appendix (c). One of his best compositions is also his last, the Elégie, opus 47, published in 1881. Schafhäutl, in his "Life of Boehm," speaks thus of it: "His swan-song bears the very characteristic title of 'Elégie.' It is written in the key of A♭ major; a sweet melancholy rises through forty bars to a bitter lamentation, only to sink back by degrees to a peaceful resignation. It is the aged man, who, already ailing, once said in his eighty-seventh year: 'I would that I might yet live to the ninetieth year; but as God wills.' The Elégie is composed for full orchestra. The orchestra raises the composition to a work of true magnificence, developing here and there, in a most effective way, what the singing flute-voice only suggests."]

FIG. 46.
The house at 20 Altheimereck, Munich, where Boehm lived

FIG. 47.
Inner court, looking toward Boehm's home and shop

APPENDIX

(a) Biographical Notes

Theobald Boehm was born in Munich, Bavaria, on April 9, 1794. He was born, lived, worked, and died in the same house, at No. 20 *Altheimereck.* The Boehm family occupied a flat in a building which had once formed part of one of the religious houses in which before the suppression of such institutions in Bavaria, Munich abounded. It had been the residence of Boehm's father, and his descendants continued to live there. Fig. 46 shows this house, as seen from the street, from a photograph taken by the translator in 1905. The entrance (in the center, at the left of the lamp post) leads into the inner court, and from this court there are various doors and stairways leading to numerous apartments which constitute the building as a whole. Fig. 47 is a view taken in this inner court, looking toward Boehm's apartment. The family lived on the third floor, and the workshops of "Th. Boehm & Mendler" were on the fourth floor just over the living rooms. He was married in 1820. In 1870 there was a celebration of the Golden Wedding, with a family consisting of seven sons, one daughter, seven daughters-in-law, and thirty grandchildren. Boehm died on November 25, 1881, in his eighty-eighth year. In this house on April 9, 1894, there was held a family celebration to commemorate the centenary of Boehm's birth.

Professor Dr. Carl von Schafhäutl, of the University of Munich, was a life-long friend and companion of Boehm, having lived for years in Boehm's home. In 1882 Schafhäutl wrote a series of articles entitled, "Theobald Boehm: The Life of a Remarkable Artist," which appeared in the *Allgemeine Musikalische Zeitung* of Leipzig. A translation of this life of Boehm is given in Welch's "History of the Boehm Flute," and fills 102 pages. Welch also gives a "Memoir of Dr. Schafhäutl" which fills 24 pages.

In 1909, as stated in the Preface, the translator received from Mr. James S. Wilkins, Jr., an account of Boehm's life-work written by Mr. Wilkins in 1900. This gives the impressions of Boehm's personal characteristics as received by an American pupil who was closely associated with Boehm for more than three years, and it also gives some opinions expressed by Boehm which have not been found elsewhere. Extracts from this account are therefore given here; the parts omitted are mostly descriptions of Boehm's experiments and conclusions which are given by Boehm himself in this treatise, and accounts of his work in connection with the iron and steel industry, which are given in full by Schafhäutl.

THEOBALD BOEHM—AN APPRECIATION
by
JAMES S. WILKINS, JR.
1900

It was the good fortune of the writer to become the pupil of Theobald Boehm in May, 1871, and to enjoy the inestimable honor of being made a close friend and companion by him for more than three years.

During the writer's sojourn in Munich, he translated into English Mr. Boehm's work on the flute, "Die Flöte und das Flötenspiel" (which remained in Boehm's possession, unpublished). It was suggested at this time that Mr. Boehm's biography would be of interest as an introduction to the translation, but he was opposed to this. His life was devoted to study and investigation, carried out in the systematic manner so characteristic of the German student and scholar. He was naturally modest and of a retiring nature; his was a character that could not tolerate superficiality or ostentation.

It is only with a desire to give to the lovers of the flute and to admirers of the man who created such a revolution in the instrument, a clearer understanding of the one who has accomplished this result, and to set forth the character of this truly great man, that this sketch of his life is now written.

* * *

Mr. Boehm was about 5 feet, 10 inches in height, of well knit frame and strong constitution. His eyes were a striking feature; they were brown in color, of a wonderful brightness and intelligence, and beaming with kindness. He was full of genial, quiet humor, but with the air of energy and determination which his life bore out. He was highly cultured and had a fund of interesting reminiscence rarely met with.

He was ever ready to encourage the ambitious scholar with advice and assistance, and he did so in a manner to win him the admiration, love, and respect of all with whom he came in contact. It was instinctive with him to bring out all the best qualities of his pupils. His was a great nature—full of charity and human kindness.

As an illustration of Mr. Boehm's method I may give a personal incident. I learned to play all of Boehm's compositions in concert, from memory; in fact, at the close of my three years of study with him, I had a repertoire of 500 solos, memorized! I went to 20 *Altheimereck* every day, at 9 o'clock, a. m., Mr. Boehm would say to me: "I have a new piece"—placing it on the music stand and giving *tempo*—"play it." When I had finished the last page, he would turn the music upside down, and repeat: "Play it." This meant that I should play all that I could remember. In this way I became able to memorize a piece at first reading, and it also taught me to read many bars ahead.

Mr. Boehm's school of tone stands supreme, and his pupils have demonstrated this fact. With him tone was of the first importance, all else became secondary; and, while the development of tone meant drudgery, yet the results compensated for all the labor entailed.

* * *

All this time the natural obstacles to the creation of a perfect flute confronted Mr. Boehm. The human hands have but ten fingers and the musical scale has thirteen tones, and the proper operation of the flute could only be accomplished by mechanical means. For years Mr. Boehm labored on this problem and the hundreds of designs he made in experimentation can hardly be realized. He continued the experiments until he reluctantly decided that any device that could be created for an ideal flute would be so complicated and so subject to disarrangement that it would be impractical. The present flute is not perfect, and Mr. Boehm fully realized this fact. The creation of a mechanism of easy and simple operation, the adoption of dimensions best suited to the scope of the instrument required that some of the tone-holes be located out of their correct acoustical positions. They were established only by experiment. It is impossible to have an adequate realization of the immense amount of labor Mr. Boehm devoted to the determination of such proportions as have given us the wonderful flute that we now have. None but a person of his character would have devoted a life-time to the accomplishment of his ideals.

The writer with the approval of Mr. Boehm worked nine months in his flute factory and learned the practical making of the instrument. Consequently he had many conversations with his preceptor on the reasons that influenced him to establish the present construction of the flute as the most feasible. One of the greatest difficulties he had to contend with was the opposition that players of the old flute had to any innovation or change.

* * *

The tone-holes of wooden flutes are smaller than those made of metal, because of the counter-boring for the pad seats in the former, while the metal flutes have raised edges around the holes. The ideal flute is one of wood with raised tone-holes. The wood of the main part of the tube being cut away for lightness; this permits using full-sized tone-holes. Mr. Boehm did make some few flutes of this kind, and they were splendid instruments, but the greatly increased cost and the danger of splitting made them too expensive, and few players appreciated the real advantages to be derived from their use. (The bass flute tube shown in Fig. 31, presented by Mr. Wilkins, shows such a "thinned wood" tube).

* * *

When he was about sixty years of age Mr. Boehm created his *Alt-Flöte in G.* This was the pride of his life, and during the last twenty years of his life he played on this instrument altogether. The principal obstacle to the popularity of this flute is the fact that no music is arranged for it. It is to be regretted that so little is known of this magnificent instrument.

* * *

One of the great drawbacks to the early adoption of the Boehm System by flute players was the changing of the fingering from the old to the new; this was particularly true as regards the closed G♯ key. The fallacy of the closed G♯ key, strange to say, prevails at the present time to no small extent. Even pupils are taught the false fingering by their teachers who happen themselves to use the old style. This was extremely annoying to Mr. Boehm, who remarked: "If a player goes to the trouble of changing his instrument and system of fingering he should not do so in part. The natural action of the pressing down of the finger on a key is to close the key. Then why, when no mechanical reason prevents, should this G♯ key be left to the unreliable force of a spring to close it, when the direct pressure of the finger will act so positively?" In later years Mr. Boehm would not humor this absurd notion and he refused to make the closed G♯ key for any one.

*   *   *

It was always Mr. Boehm's hope that the tone qualities and possibilities of the flute could be realized as part of the orchestral forces. He maintained that the first two octaves contain the true and natural qualities of the instrument. The third octave is always unsatisfactory; it is seldom that a player who has a fine quality of tone in the third octave, has an equally excellent lower tone, and conversely. Therefore it was Mr. Boehm's wish to create an orchestral set of flutes, composed of flutes in G, in C, and in F, each designed to have a compass of two octaves of the ideal tone quality. But as this would increase the number of flute players in the orchestra there is hardly any possibility of its realization; not that it is impossible but because there is a general indifference to the question.

It is evident from the character of the music at present available for the flute, that very little of it is composed with a full comprehension of the character of the instrument. The prevailing music is nearly all of a florid nature, quite foreign to the acoustical quality of the flute. There is no question that the third octave is false and thin as compared with the lower ones, and, in fact, these

lower octaves are purposely injured in order to develop
the third or artificial octave. (See page 19. These arguments do not apply to the flute in G made on Boehm's
dimensions). The proof of this fact is found in the
irregular fingering that must be used to produce the third
octave. The elimination of the effort to produce three
full octaves of tones would permit the development of
the full, rich tone of the two lower octaves which give
the qualities that tend to make the flute the beautiful
instrument that it is. Development along these natural
lines is the ideal to be sought.

* * *

Mr. Boehm had seven sons and one daughter, and once
when speaking of his family, said: "I have raised a good
family and have given them all a good education to fit
them to make their way in the world." This was true;
one son became Manager of the Bavarian State Railways,
another Manager of a locomotive factory, a third Manager
of the Stuttgart gas works, one was secretary to Prince
Charles, two held positions of trust in municipal of-
fices in Munich, and one carried on the family business
of goldsmith and jeweler, all being men of prominent
position in their communities. The daughter never married and lived at home.

Mr. Boehm's affliction in later years was the failure of
his eye-sight. This was not caused alone by advancing
years, but was the result mainly of the years of hard
work spent in experiments in making steel from iron
directly. The constant watching of the metal and the
heat of the intense fires seriously affected his eyes.

* * *

It was remarkable that a man who had been so active
as Mr. Boehm had been for many years, should retain
his faculties in such a marked degree to the time of his
death. In 1872, when he was in his seventy-seventh year,
he was as companionable as the average man of sixty
years, and his mind was as bright. This was probably
due to the well regulated life he led. Until his death, in
1881, he always dwelt upon the improvement of the flute
or upon the arrangement of some music for it.

* * *

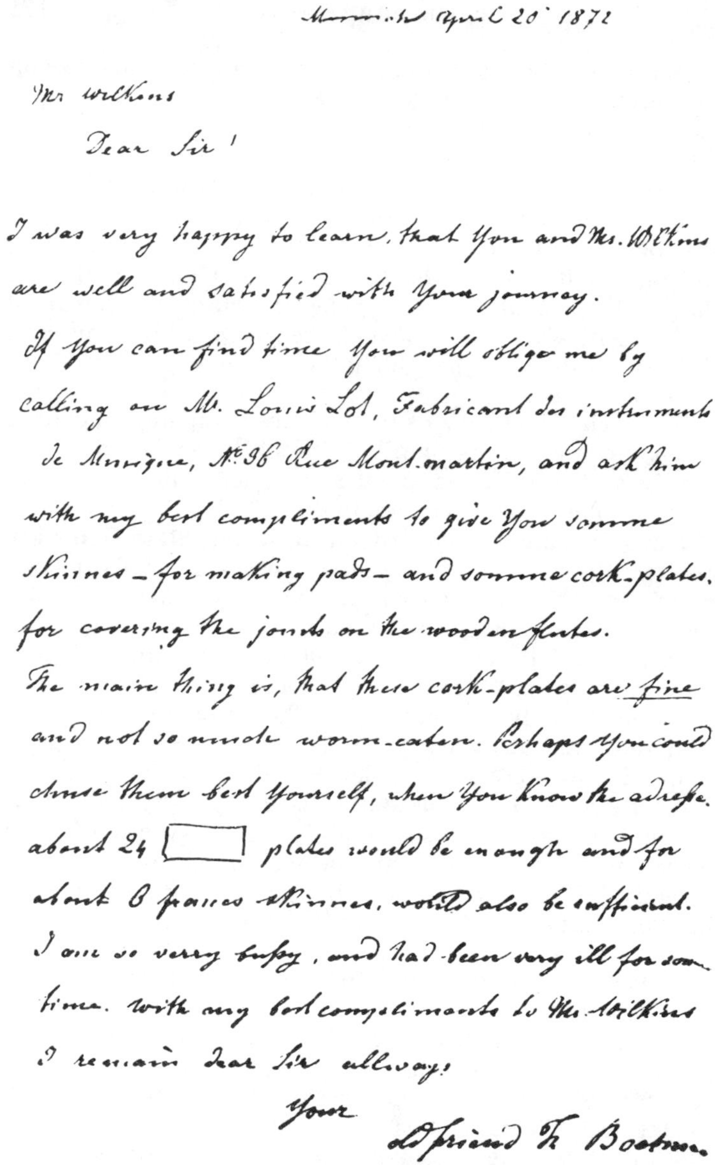

Munich April 20ᵗʰ 1872

Mr Wilkins

    Dear Sir!

I was very happy to learn, that You and Mrs. Wilkins
are well and satisfied with Your journey.
If You can find time You will oblige me by
calling on Mr. Louis Lot, Fabricant des instruments
de Musique, N° 36 Rue Mont-martin, and ask him
with my best compliments to give You somme
skinnes – for making pads – and somme cork-plates,
for covering the joints on the wooden flutes.
The main thing is, that these cork-plates are _fine_
and not so much worm-eaten. Perhaps You could
chuse them best Yourself, when You know the adresse.
about 24 ☐ plates would be enough and for
about 8 francs skinnes, would also be sufficient.
I am so very busy, and had been very ill for som
time. With my best compliments to Mrs. Wilkins
I remain Dear Sir allways

      Your
         old friend Th. Boehm

Fig. 48. Facsimile of a letter in Boehm's handwriting.

A letter written by Boehm to Mr. Wilkins when the latter was visiting Paris, is reproduced in fac-simile on the opposite page. This letter throws an interesting side-light upon Boehm's personal quali-ties. While there are traces of his multi-lingual accomplishments, yet it shows that he was very competent in English composition, and it shows him to be the man of courtesy and culture to which Mr. Wilkins and others have abundantly attested. Mr. Wilkins was accompanied by his mother during his stay in Europe, and it is to her that Boehm refers in the opening and closing sen-tences.

Boehm's researches in acoustics, while mostly applicable to the flute, are fundamental, and they have influenced the development of other wind in-struments with keys, such as the clarinet, oboe, bassoon, etc. Some features of Boehm's key mech-anism are in general use with these instruments, and are referred to by his name. The location of the holes, however, cannot be carried out for these instruments, according to the *Schema,* be-cause of the modifying influence of the reed.

Boehm's attempt, in 1831, to improve the piano-forte shows that he approached the subject in a thoroughly rational manner; his method was cor-rect, and is now universally adopted; he failed temporarily, because he had no facilities to carry on the work. The *Encyclopaedia Britannica,* 11th edition, article "Pianoforte," says, "The first sug-gestion for the overstringing in the piano, was made by the celebrated flute-player and inventor

Theobald Boehm, who carried it beyond theory in London, in 1831, by employing a small firm located in Cheapside, Gerock & Wolf, to make some overstrung pianos for him. Boehm expected to gain in tone. Pape, an ingenious mechanician in Paris, tried a like experiment to gain economy in dimensions. Tomkinson in London continued Pape's model, but neither Boehm's nor Pape's took permanent root. Later in 1855, Henry Engelhard Steinway, who had emigrated from Brunswick to New York in 1849, and had established the firm of Steinway & Sons in 1853 in that city, effected a combination of an overstrung scale with the American iron frame * * * leading ultimately to important results. The Chickering firm claim to have anticipated the Steinways in this invention."

Boehm devised a new method of transmitting rotatory motion. A model of this was presented before the Society of Arts, Manufactures and Commerce, of London, and on June 8, 1835, the president of the Society, the Duke of Sussex, presented Boehm with the Silver Medal of the Society. The record is found in the *Transactions* of the Society, Vol. L, Part II, for the Session 1834-35, pages 82 and 83. It begins as follows: "Method of Communicating Rotatory Motion. The Silver Medal was presented to Mr. Theobald Boehm, member of the Royal Chapel at Munich, in Bavaria, for his Method of Communicating Rotatory Motion; a Model of which has been placed in the Society's Repository. The usual modes of communicating rotatory motion from the first mover, are by means either of wheels and pinions, or of two plane cylinders connected by a band. Mr. Boehm has suggested another method, described in the annexed figures." Then follows a technical description of the figures; these figures are reproduced in Fig. 49, from which the nature of the device can be easily inferred, without further description.

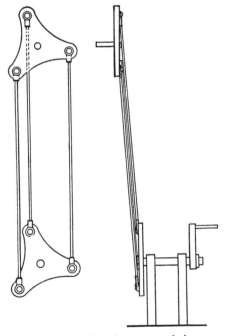

FIG. 49. Device for transmitting rotatory motion.

Boehm received many medals, decorations, and prizes. Mr. Welch says: "So many prize medals and similar distinctions did he succeed in obtaining, that he had a drawer specially devoted to them. The old man seemed quite pleased when, only a few weeks before his death, he opened it and showed me his trophies." He received three Grand First Prize Gold Medals for his flutes, at the London Exhibition of 1851, at the German Industrial Exhibition, Munich, in 1854, and at the Paris Exhibition of 1855. In 1835 he was awarded the Silver Medal of the Society of Arts of London for the method of transmitting rotatory motion, described in the preceding paragraph. In 1839 the King of Bavaria bestowed the Cross of the Knights of the Order of Merit of St. Michael, for Boehm's introduction into the iron-works of Bavaria of improved puddling processes for the manufacture of steel.

PREIS-COURANT

von

Theobald Böhm & Mendler in München.

		Mark	Pf
No. I. Eine Silberflöte (in C) mit Embouchure von Gold . .		410	-
Dito mit H-Fuss		450	-
II. Flöte von Cocus- oder Grenadille-Holz mit Silber .		375	-
Dito mit H-Fuss		410	-
„ III. Holzflöte mit Neusilber		300	-
„ IV. Flöte von Neusilber mit Holz-Embouchure			
„ V. Eine Altflöte (in G) von Silber mit Gold-Embouchure		630	-
Dito von Neusilber mit Holz-Embouchure . . .		450	-
„ VI. Piccolo von Silber mit Holz-Embouchure . .		300	-
Dito von Holz mit Silber		250	-
Dito von Holz mit Neusilber			

Zu den Flöten No. I und II wird auf Verlangen noch gemacht:

a) Ein Trillerhebel zur $\overset{2}{C}$-Klappe . . . . $\qquad$ 24 -

*b) Eine Schleifklappe . . . . $\qquad$ 18 -

c) Federn von Gold . . . . $\qquad$ 18 -

Requisiten: Eine Garnitur Klappenpolster . . . . . $\qquad$ 3 -

Schraubenzieher und Federnhäckchen . . . . $\qquad$ 3 -

Stopselmass . . . . $\qquad$ 1 -

Grifftabelle . . . . $\qquad$ 3 -

Emballage mit Holzkistchen . . . . . . $\qquad$ 2 -

Bemerkungen. * Mittelst der sehr bequemen Schleifklappe können die Töne:
$\overset{2}{dis}$-$\overset{2}{es}$. $\overset{3}{d}$, $\overset{3}{dis}$-$\overset{3}{es}$, $\overset{3}{e}$, $\overset{3}{a}$ und $\overset{3}{b}$, auch im Pianissimo vollkommen rein und sicher gespielt werden.

Versendungen werden nur gegen erfolgte Baarzahlungen oder Wechsel auf bekannte deutsche Bankhäuser gemacht.

FIG. 50. A facsimile of Boehm and Mendler's Price List of Flutes, of the year 1877.

(b) Descriptive Price List of Boehm & Mendler Flutes

The manuscript copy of "Die Flöte und das Flötenspiel" concludes with a descriptive catalogue of the various styles of flutes manufactured by Boehm & Mendler. This part, however, has been crossed out, indicating Boehm's decision not to publish it. In the translator's collection there are several of the original price-lists of Boehm & Mendler and of Carl Mendler; a photographic reproduction of one of these is shown in Fig. 50. This was sent, in 1877, by Boehm himself to Mr. Chaffee of Detroit, who purchased the flute described in the Group, Fig. 31, No. 11. Shafhäutl's "Life of Boehm," in the German edition, gives a catalogue, which is much the same as Boehm's list, except that it is more detailed and is expressed in language almost naïve. Since the English version of Schafhäutl's "Life" does not contain this matter, it is given below, with the addition of a few minor items for the sake of completeness, taken from a Carl Mendler price-list.

Herr Carl Mendler, who took over Boehm's flute-making establishment in 1862, continues the manufacture of the Boehm flutes in all their newest developments.

A flute in C of cocus or grenadilla wood with silver keys is provided for 375 marks. If one wishes a B♮ foot-joint, the price is increased to 410 marks; while if the foot descends only to D♮ the price of the flute is but 320 marks.

With this flute there is furnished an elegant case, which contains not only the flute, but also the necessary tools with which to take the flute apart when the mechanism needs cleaning, or a key pad needs changing, or, perchance, to remedy some disturbance in the operation of the mechanism. These requisites consist of: one set of key pads, 3 marks; a screw driver with a spring hook, 3 marks; a stopper measure by which the cork can be replaced in the correct position, 1 mark; tables of fingerings, 3 marks; cost of packing the flute in a wooden box, 2 marks. These items together amount to 12 marks.

An extra foot-joint to B♮ costs 95 marks, one to C costs 65 marks, and one to D♮ only costs 30 marks. An extra head-joint of silver or of wood costs 50 marks.

A flute in C, of silver with gold embouchure, costs 410 marks. The same instrument with a B♮ foot-joint is 450 marks, or with a D♮ foot it is 360 marks.

The same flute of the newest system with a large diameter of bore, 20 millimeters, giving a fuller tone, with a foot to C, costs 485 marks, or with a foot to B♮ the price is 525 marks.

There is still Boehm's latest improvement, the above silver flute of 20 millimeters bore with a head-joint of grenadilla wood, the price of which is 475 marks with a C foot, or 515 marks with a B♮ foot. By means of this head-joint of wood, the flute acquires the character of tone of the wood flute.

In accordance with the old system of flute, and especially to conform to the French style, there will be supplied, instead of the Boehm open G♯ key, a closed G♯ key at an extra cost of 20 marks. One may also have a trill lever for the C key (thumb key) which can be played by the first finger of the right hand; Mendler furnishes this for 24 marks.

Mendler also provides his flutes with the octave-key by which certain tones can easily and surely be produced in *pianissimo*. The price of this is 18 marks.

If one wishes gold springs instead of steel springs, the extra cost is 18 marks. And little gold plates may be put on the keys where the fingers press, for 50 marks.

A flute of cocus or grenadilla wood with keys of German silver, with steel springs, open G♯ key and C foot, costs 300 marks; with B♮ foot, 320 marks, and with foot to D♮, 270 marks.

A bass flute in G (Alt-Flöte) of silver with a gold embouchure costs 650 marks. A similar flute of German silver with an embouchure of wood costs only 450 marks.

A piccolo of silver with embouchure of wood costs 300 marks, while the price of a piccolo made of cocus or grenadilla wood, with keys of silver, is 250 marks.

Unless it is otherwise desired, all of these flutes are provided with the thumb rest (the crutch for the left hand).

These prices may seem high; however, it is not possible, because of the complicated and delicate mechanism, to secure its accurate working by means of the cheaper workmanship. The correct adjustment of this complicated mechanism requires the skill of an exceptional mechanic. Boehm had at one time a mechanic from the celebrated workshop of Ertel, but his work was not sufficiently accurate. The same was the case with a mechanic from the celebrated optical establishment of Merz.

It was not until the year 1854, when the present proprietor of the factory, the exceptionally skilled watchmaker, Carl Mendler, became foreman, that it was possible to make the mechanism of the required perfection.

Flutes on Boehm's system are to be found in the market at cheaper prices; but one must not be misled; the closing of the keys, for example, will be very imperfect, or the flute itself will be unmanageable, and the instrument will be found more often in the hands of the repairer than in those of the artist.

(c) LIST OF BOEHM'S COMPOSITIONS

Schafhäutl in his "Life of Boehm" (Welch: "History of the Boehm Flute"), gives a list of Boehm's compositions, prepared from his personal papers. In this list there are numerous errors and omissions. The translator's collection contains copies, in the original editions, of all of Boehm's published compositions and arrangements (excepting Op. 14). The following list gives the complete titles as they appear on the printed music. Wherever this list differs from that of Schafhäutl and Welch this one may be taken as correct. In the absence of other information, Schafhäutl has been followed.

Schafhäutl, in the German edition, gives the following sentences as an introduction to the List of Compositions: "In order that our picture of the man whose methods and works we have followed through various fields of human endeavor, may be made complete and well filled-out, we must also keep in view the man as an artist in his creations. From his first composition, which appeared in the year 1822, to his last which was published in 1881, there flows continuously the living spirit; and even in the most difficult etudes for the virtuoso there is always a vivifying musical thought. Throughout all of his many-sided compositions for the flute, we find that he holds truly and steadfastly to an aesthetic unity which gives them an enduring value."

When a title in the following list is followed by an asterisk, *, it signifies that there is an accompaniment for the pianoforte; two asterisks, **, signify an accompaniment for the pianoforte and also for the orchestra; the obelisk, †, indicates that the accompaniment is for the orchestra only; the absence of a mark indicates that the composition is for the flute alone.

I. ORIGINAL COMPOSITIONS WITH OPUS NUMBERS

Opus	Date	Title	Key	
1	1822	Concerto pour la Flûte, dédié à Monsieur A. B. Fürstenau ____	G maj.	* *
2		La Sentinelle Air Favori Varié dédié a son Elève Monsieur Guillaume Zink _____	G maj.	* *
3		Andante und Polonaise_____ _____A maj. and	D maj.	* *
4		Nel cor più non mi sento, thême varié _____	G maj.	* *
5		P o t p o u r i sur des Mélodies Suisses, Duo concertant _____	G maj.	*
6		Divertissement sur un Air de Caraffa, dédié à Monsieur de Manostetter _____	G maj.	* *
7		Concertante pour deux Flûtes, (with orchestral accompaniment only) _____	G maj.	†
8		Polonaise de Caraffa _____	D maj.	* *
9		Variations sur un thême de l'Opera: Robin-de-Bois (Der Freyschütz) de Weber, dédiées à son ami Fr. Hoffmann_____	D maj.	* *
10		Divertissement sur un thême favori de Rovelli dédié à Monsieur Krüger _____	D maj.	* *
11		Divertissement sur deux thêmes favoris suisses _____C maj. and	G maj.	* *
12		Rondo Brilliant, dédié à Son Ami Charles Keller, (with orchestral accompaniment only)	D maj.	†

13		Divertissement sur l'air favori intitulé Almalied, par Baron de Poissl introduit dans l'Opera Donauweibchen, dédié à Son Eleve Monsieur David Marx _____	G maj.	* *
14		"Boehm et Ogden." Fantaisie concert sur un thême ecossais	D maj.	*
15		12 Etudes pour la Flûte, propres à égaliser le doigté dans toutes les gammes _____		
16		Grande Polonaise, dediée à Monsieur Camus _____	D maj.	* *
17		Variations sur la marche de l'Opera Moisé, dediées à Monsieur Tulou _____	D maj.	* *
18		I—Erstes W a l z e r Potpourri, nach Franz Schubert'schen und anderen beliebten Motiven _____(various)		*
		II—Andante und Polonaise nach Motiven von Caraffa. Dedicated to Mr. Alfred Croshaw Johnson _____(various)		*
19		Choix d'Airs de l'Opera "Macbeth" par A. H. Chelard_____		*
20	1838	Variations sur un Air Tyrolien (Swiss Boy) dédiées à Monsieur Prosper Amtmann_____	C maj.	* *
21	1838	Fantaisie sur un air de Beethoven. (Sehnsuchtswalzer) ___	Ab maj.	* *
22	1840	Variations brillantes sur l'air allemand "Du, du liegst mir im Herzen" _____	E maj.	* *
23	1845	Fantaisie sur des thêmes suisses. dediée à Mr. J. Clinton_____	F maj.	* *
24	1845	Fantaisie sur des thêmes suisses dediée à Mr. L. Dorus _____	E maj.	* *
25	1852	Fantaisie sur des airs écossais	C maj.	* *
26	1852	Twenty-four Capricios, dedicated to Edward Jekyll, Esqre.		
27	1853	Souvenir des Alpes; I. Andante cantabile _____	Eb maj.	*

28	1853	Souvenir des Alpes; II. Rondo-Allegro	C maj.	*
29	1853	Souvenir des Alpes; III. Andantino, Romance	D maj.	*
30	1853	Souvenir des Alpes; IV. Rondo-Allegretto	D maj.	*
31	1853	Souvenir des Alpes; V. Andante pastorale	G maj.	*
32	1853	Souvenir des Alpes; VI. Rondo-Ländler	E maj.	*
33	1858	Andante	B maj.	*
34	1859	A la Tarantella, dediée à Monsieur Antoine Sacchetti	E min.	*
35	1859	Larghetto, dedié à Monsieur Louis Dorus	A♭ maj.	*
36	1859	Rondo à la Mazurka	C maj.	*
37	1863	24 Etudes, avec accomp. de Piano. En 4 Suites		*
38				
39				
40				
41				
42				
43				
44				
45	1876	Fantasie über Motive einer Sonate von F. H. Himmel, à Hernn Camille Thierry (This work appears as No. 12 in the list, II, of "Compositionen berühmter Meister," and bears the opus number on the first page of music and not on the title page.)	C maj.	*
46	1880	Andante aus der Serenade, Op. 25, von L. van Beethoven. To Herrn Eugen Weiner in New York	G maj.	*
47	1881	Elégie, dediée à Monsieur le Dr. F. Jsenschmid	A♭ maj.	* *

1-13   Vollständige Sammlung der Con-
            cert Compositionen für die
            Flöte mit Hinweglassung der
            Begleitung. (Contains solo
            parts only of Op. 1 to 13 in-
            clusive, with the exception of
            Op. 5.)

II. TRANSCRIPTIONS WITHOUT OPUS NUMBERS

This group of transcriptions for the flute and piano
appears under the general title: *Compositionen berühm-
ter Meister.*

No.	Date	Title	Key	
1	1872	Adagio, (Largo, Pianoforte Con-certo, Op. 15), von L. v. Beethoven	C maj.	*
2	1872	Adagio, von Mozart. Aus der Clavier-Sonate Op. 16	Bb maj.	*
3	1872	Rondo-Andante von Mozart	A min.	*
4	1872	Ständchen. Lied von Franz Schubert	D min.	*
5	1872	Das Fischermädchen. Lied von Franz Schubert	D maj.	*
6	1872	Tre giorni. Aria von Pergolese	C min.	*
7	1872	Cantabile von Vogler	D maj.	*
8	1872	Aria cantabile von J. S. Bach	D maj.	*
9	1876	Marcia, Adagio, Menuetto, Alle-gretto alla Polacca und Tema con Variazioni aus L. v. Beethoven's Serenade Op. 8. (Original for Violin, Viola and Violincello.) Gerwidmit Herrn M. Schweninger	D maj.	*
10	1876	Romanze von L. v. Beethoven, Op. 50	F maj.	*
11	1876	Variationen von Haydn über das Thema: Gott erhalte Franz den Kaiser	G maj.	*

(The List printed on the cover of the music of this
series contains twelve numbers, but No. 12 is clearly
marked "Opus 45," and is now entered in group I only.)

III. MISCELLANEOUS WORKS WITHOUT NUMBERS

There is no available record of the titles to which Boehm intended to attach the seven opus numbers from 38 to 44, inclusive. There remain just seven published works which bear no opus or serial numbers, and whose dates of publication correspond with those appropriate to the missing opera. It is suggested that these works are the ones which should bear the opus numbers from 38 to 44, inclusive:

No.	Opus	Date	Title	Key	
1	(38)	1863	Andante de Mozart, Op. 86. (Arranged from the original MS. score, for the flute and piano, and for the flute in G and piano)	C maj.	*
2	(39)	1868	Arie aus Orpheus: "Che faro senza Euridice," von Gluck. Au Colonel Comte A. Vargas de Bedemar _____	Eb maj.	*
3	(40)	1868	Cujus Animam. Célèbre Air du Stabat Mater de Rossini. Dedié à Mr. Hermann Kohlke _____	Ab maj.	*
4	(41)	1871	12 Uebungstücke für die Flöte zur Erlangung einer gleichmässigen Fingerbewegung in allen Tonarten. Zugleich als Anhang zu dessen theor. Werke: Die Flöte und das Flötenspiel in akustischer, technischer und artistischer Beziehung__		
5	(42)	1876	Adagio aus dem Quintetto für Clarinette von Mozart _____	G maj.	*
6	(43)		3 Duos pour deux Flûtes tirés des oeuvres de F. Mendelssohn Bartholdy et de Fr. Lachner. No. 1. Sur Melodies de Mendelssohn _____	Bb maj.	*

No. 2.   Sur   Melodies   de
Mendelssohn _____ E♭ maj.   *
No. 3.   Sur   Melodies   de
Lachner _____ F maj.   *
(This series of three duets,
published   in   Paris,   is
clearly   marked   "Opus
33."   Possibly   this   is   a
misprint for "Opus 43.")

7   (44)   "My Native Home." (Sehn-
sucht   nach   dem   Rigi.)
Song with flute obbligato.

IV.   Unpublished Arrangements for the Flute in G

There is no evidence that there are any unpublished
original compositions by Boehm.   The group of pieces
listed below consists of arrangements with parts for the
flute in G.   In nearly all of the numbers, the "arrange·
ment" seemingly required is merely the transposition
of a part into a suitable key for the flute in G.   The list
is very interesting as indicating the selections which
Boehm had found especially adapted to this instrument.
The publication of these works at the present time, in
"album" form, might stimulate the interest in this beautiful instrument.

The keys in this list are those given by Schafhäutl.
These would indicate that in some instances the solo part
has been transposed, while in other cases it is the accompaniment that has been rewritten.   Twelve of the
numbers seem to be the same compositions as are represented by twelve of the published works; the numbers in
parenthesis refer to the corresponding groups and numbers.

For Flute in G and Pianoforte

No.	Title	Key
1	Beethoven. Adagio. Largo from the Piano-forte Concerto, Op. 15. (II-1) _____	A♭ maj.
2	Beethoven. Sonata, Op. 17. The original for Horn and Pianoforte _____	F maj.
3	Beethoven. Serenade, Op. 25. The original for Flute, Violin and Viola. (I-Op. 46) ___	
4	Haydn. Variations on "God Preserve the Emperor." The original for String Quar-tette. (II-11) _____	

5 Himmel. Rondo. From a Sonata originally
   for Flute and Pianoforte. (I-Op. 45, and
   II-12) ------------------------------------ G maj.
6 Mozart. Adagio. From the Pianoforte Sonata, Op. 16. (II-2) --------------------- B♭ maj.
7 Mozart. Rondo Andante, Op. 71. The original for the Pianoforte alone. (II-3) -----
8 Mozart. Sonata. The original for Violin
   and Pianoforte ------------------------- G maj.
9 Mozart. Adagio from the Clarinet Quintette.
   (III-5) ----------------------------------- D maj.
10 Schubert. Song: "Das Ständchen." (Ser-
    enade.) (II-5) ----------------------- D min.
11 Schubert. Song: "Das Fischermädchen."
    (II-5) ----------------------------------- A maj.
12 Schubert. Song: "Am Meer." ------------ C maj.
13 Vogler. Cantabile. Adagio from an Organ
    Prelude. (II-7) ---------------------- D min.

DUETS FOR FLUTE IN G AND FLUTE IN C, WITH PIANOFORTE

14 Rossini. Duo: Soirées Musicales --------- A maj.
15 Rossini. Duo: Soirées Musicales --------- D maj.
16 Weber. Romance ----------------------- F maj.
17 Weber. Andantino --------------------- C maj.
18 Weber. Allegretto -------------------- C maj.

TRIOS FOR FLUTE IN G AND TWO FLUTES IN C

19 Beethoven. Trio, Op. 87. The original for
    two Oboes and Cor Anglais ------------ F maj.
20 Vogler. Cantabile. Adagio from an Organ
    Prelude. (II-7, and IV-6) -------------- D maj.

FOR FLUTE IN G AND SOPRANO VOICE, WITH
ACCOMPANIMENT

21 Scheidemayer. Graduale. With Latin text
    for church use, and also with German text.
    With Pianoforte accompaniment_____ C maj.
22 Walter. Graduale. For Solo Flute in G,
    Vocal Quartette, and accompaniment for
    two Violins, Viola, Cello and Bass_____ E maj.

(d) BIBLIOGRAPHY

There follows a very brief and incomplete list of current books relating to the flute. Older treatises of historical value, instructors, books of music, and books treating of musical instruments in general have not been included. More extended bibliographies are given by Rockstro, Welch, and Fitzgibbon, in the works mentioned below.

BOEHM, THEOBALD.—An Essay on the Construction of Flutes. Edited by W. S. Broadwood. This book is Boehm's own English version of his treatise of 1847, *Ueber den Flötenbau und die neuesten Verbesserungen desselben,* to which the editor has added an account of the *Schema,* and numerous letters of interest. London: Rudall, Carte & Co., 1882. Octavo, X + 78 pages.

ROCKSTRO, R. S.—A Treatise on the Construction, the History, and the Practice of the Flute. London: Rudall, Carte & Co., 1890. Octavo, XLII + 664 pages.

WELCH, CHRISTOPHER.—History of the Boehm Flute, with Schafhäutl's Life of Boehm. London: Rudall, Carte & Co.; New York, G. Schirmer; 3rd edition, 1896. Octavo, XXIII + 504 pages.

FITZGIBBON, H. MACAULAY.—The Story of the Flute. London, Walter Scott Publishing Co.; New York, Charles Scribner's Sons. 1914. Duodecimo, XVI + 292 pages.

WELCH, CHRISTOPHER.—Six Lectures on the Recorder and Other Flutes in Relation to Literature. London: Oxford University Press, 1911. Octavo, XVI + 457 pages.

EHRLICH, D.—The History of the Flute. New York: D. Ehrlich, 1921. Duodecimo, XI + 107 pages.

SCHWEDLER, MAXIMILIAN.—Katechismus der Flöte und des Flötenspiels. Leipzig: J. J. Weber, 3rd edition, 1914. Sexto-decimo, 112 pages and tables.

SQUARZONI, FRANCESCO.—Il Flauto, Cenno Storico. Ferrara, Italia, G. Bresciani. 1917. Octavo, 48 pages.

THE FLUTIST.—A monthly magazine devoted exclusively to the flute and flute playing. It is of interest and value, alike to the professional and the amateur flutist. Edited and published by EMIL MEDICUS, Asheville, North Carolina.

INDEX

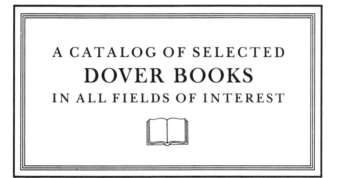

A CATALOG OF SELECTED
DOVER BOOKS
IN ALL FIELDS OF INTEREST

A CATALOG OF SELECTED DOVER
BOOKS IN ALL FIELDS OF INTEREST

DRAWINGS OF REMBRANDT, edited by Seymour Slive. Updated Lippmann, Hofstede de Groot edition, with definitive scholarly apparatus. All portraits, biblical sketches, landscapes, nudes. Oriental figures, classical studies, together with selection of work by followers. 550 illustrations. Total of 630pp. 9⅛ × 12¼.
21485-0, 21486-9 Pa., Two-vol. set $29.90

GHOST AND HORROR STORIES OF AMBROSE BIERCE, Ambrose Bierce. 24 tales vividly imagined, strangely prophetic, and decades ahead of their time in technical skill: "The Damned Thing," "An Inhabitant of Carcosa," "The Eyes of the Panther," "Moxon's Master," and 20 more. 199pp. 5⅜ × 8½. 20767-6 Pa. $3.95

ETHICAL WRITINGS OF MAIMONIDES, Maimonides. Most significant ethical works of great medieval sage, newly translated for utmost precision, readability. Laws Concerning Character Traits, Eight Chapters, more. 192pp. 5⅜ × 8½.
24522-5 Pa. $4.50

THE EXPLORATION OF THE COLORADO RIVER AND ITS CANYONS, J. W. Powell. Full text of Powell's 1,000-mile expedition down the fabled Colorado in 1869. Superb account of terrain, geology, vegetation, Indians, famine, mutiny, treacherous rapids, mighty canyons, during exploration of last unknown part of continental U.S. 400pp. 5⅜ × 8½. 20094-9 Pa. $7.95

HISTORY OF PHILOSOPHY, Julián Marías. Clearest one-volume history on the market. Every major philosopher and dozens of others, to Existentialism and later. 505pp. 5⅜ × 8½. 21739-6 Pa. $9.95

ALL ABOUT LIGHTNING, Martin A. Uman. Highly readable non-technical survey of nature and causes of lightning, thunderstorms, ball lightning, St. Elmo's Fire, much more. Illustrated. 192pp. 5⅜ × 8½. 25237-X Pa. $5.95

SAILING ALONE AROUND THE WORLD, Captain Joshua Slocum. First man to sail around the world, alone, in small boat. One of great feats of seamanship told in delightful manner. 67 illustrations. 294pp. 5⅜ × 8½. 20326-3 Pa. $4.95

LETTERS AND NOTES ON THE MANNERS, CUSTOMS AND CONDITIONS OF THE NORTH AMERICAN INDIANS, George Catlin. Classic account of life among Plains Indians: ceremonies, hunt, warfare, etc. 312 plates. 572pp. of text. 6⅛ × 9¼. 22118-0, 22119-9, Pa. Two-vol. set $17.90

ALASKA: The Harriman Expedition, 1899, John Burroughs, John Muir, et al. Informative, engrossing accounts of two-month, 9,000-mile expedition. Native peoples, wildlife, forests, geography, salmon industry, glaciers, more. Profusely illustrated. 240 black-and-white line drawings. 124 black-and-white photographs. 3 maps. Index. 576pp. 5⅜ × 8½. 25109-8 Pa. $11.95

THE BOOK OF BEASTS: Being a Translation from a Latin Bestiary of the Twelfth Century, T. H. White. Wonderful catalog real and fanciful beasts: manticore, griffin, phoenix, amphivius, jaculus, many more. White's witty erudite commentary on scientific, historical aspects. Fascinating glimpse of medieval mind. Illustrated. 296pp. 5⅜ × 8¼. (Available in U.S. only) 24609-4 Pa. $6.95

FRANK LLOYD WRIGHT: ARCHITECTURE AND NATURE With 160 Illustrations, Donald Hoffmann. Profusely illustrated study of influence of nature—especially prairie—on Wright's designs for Fallingwater, Robie House, Guggenheim Museum, other masterpieces. 96pp. 9¼ × 10¾. 25098-9 Pa. $7.95

FRANK LLOYD WRIGHT'S FALLINGWATER, Donald Hoffmann. Wright's famous waterfall house: planning and construction of organic idea. History of site, owners, Wright's personal involvement. Photographs of various stages of building. Preface by Edgar Kaufmann, Jr. 100 illustrations. 112pp. 9¼ × 10. 23671-4 Pa. $8.95

YEARS WITH FRANK LLOYD WRIGHT: Apprentice to Genius, Edgar Tafel. Insightful memoir by a former apprentice presents a revealing portrait of Wright the man, the inspired teacher, the greatest American architect. 372 black-and-white illustrations. Preface. Index. vi + 228pp. 8¼ × 11. 24801-1 Pa. $10.95

THE STORY OF KING ARTHUR AND HIS KNIGHTS, Howard Pyle. Enchanting version of King Arthur fable has delighted generations with imaginative narratives of exciting adventures and unforgettable illustrations by the author. 41 illustrations. xviii + 313pp. 6⅛ × 9¼. 21445-1 Pa. $6.95

THE GODS OF THE EGYPTIANS, E. A. Wallis Budge. Thorough coverage of numerous gods of ancient Egypt by foremost Egyptologist. Information on evolution of cults, rites and gods; the cult of Osiris; the Book of the Dead and its rites; the sacred animals and birds; Heaven and Hell; and more. 956pp. 6⅛ × 9¼. 22055-9, 22056-7 Pa., Two-vol. set $21.90

A THEOLOGICO-POLITICAL TREATISE, Benedict Spinoza. Also contains unfinished *Political Treatise*. Great classic on religious liberty, theory of government on common consent. R. Elwes translation. Total of 421pp. 5⅜ × 8½. 20249-6 Pa. $6.95

INCIDENTS OF TRAVEL IN CENTRAL AMERICA, CHIAPAS, AND YUCATAN, John L. Stephens. Almost single-handed discovery of Maya culture; exploration of ruined cities, monuments, temples; customs of Indians. 115 drawings. 892pp. 5⅜ × 8½. 22404-X, 22405-8 Pa., Two-vol. set $15.90

LOS CAPRICHOS, Francisco Goya. 80 plates of wild, grotesque monsters and caricatures. Prado manuscript included. 183pp. 6⅝ × 9⅝. 22384-1 Pa. $5.95

AUTOBIOGRAPHY: The Story of My Experiments with Truth, Mohandas K. Gandhi. Not hagiography, but Gandhi in his own words. Boyhood, legal studies, purification, the growth of the Satyagraha (nonviolent protest) movement. Critical, inspiring work of the man who freed India. 480pp. 5⅜ × 8½. (Available in U.S. only) 24593-4 Pa. $6.95

ILLUSTRATED DICTIONARY OF HISTORIC ARCHITECTURE, edited by Cyril M. Harris. Extraordinary compendium of clear, concise definitions for over 5,000 important architectural terms complemented by over 2,000 line drawings. Covers full spectrum of architecture from ancient ruins to 20th-century Modernism. Preface. 592pp. 7½ × 9⅝. 24444-X Pa. $15.95

THE NIGHT BEFORE CHRISTMAS, Clement Moore. Full text, and woodcuts from original 1848 book. Also critical, historical material. 19 illustrations. 40pp. 4⅝ × 6. 22797-9 Pa. $2.50

THE LESSON OF JAPANESE ARCHITECTURE: 165 Photographs, Jiro Harada. Memorable gallery of 165 photographs taken in the 1930's of exquisite Japanese homes of the well-to-do and historic buildings. 13 line diagrams. 192pp. 8⅜ × 11¼. 24778-3 Pa. $10.95

THE AUTOBIOGRAPHY OF CHARLES DARWIN AND SELECTED LETTERS, edited by Francis Darwin. The fascinating life of eccentric genius composed of an intimate memoir by Darwin (intended for his children); commentary by his son, Francis; hundreds of fragments from notebooks, journals, papers; and letters to and from Lyell, Hooker, Huxley, Wallace and Henslow. xi + 365pp. 5⅜ × 8. 20479-0 Pa. $6.95

WONDERS OF THE SKY: Observing Rainbows, Comets, Eclipses, the Stars and Other Phenomena, Fred Schaaf. Charming, easy-to-read poetic guide to all manner of celestial events visible to the naked eye. Mock suns, glories, Belt of Venus, more. Illustrated. 299pp. 5¼ × 8¼. 24402-4 Pa. $7.95

BURNHAM'S CELESTIAL HANDBOOK, Robert Burnham, Jr. Thorough guide to the stars beyond our solar system. Exhaustive treatment. Alphabetical by constellation: Andromeda to Cetus in Vol. 1; Chamaeleon to Orion in Vol. 2; and Pavo to Vulpecula in Vol. 3. Hundreds of illustrations. Index in Vol. 3. 2,000pp. 6⅛ × 9¼. 23567-X, 23568-8, 23673-0 Pa., Three-vol. set $41.85

STAR NAMES: Their Lore and Meaning, Richard Hinckley Allen. Fascinating history of names various cultures have given to constellations and literary and folkloristic uses that have been made of stars. Indexes to subjects. Arabic and Greek names. Biblical references. Bibliography. 563pp. 5⅜ × 8½. 21079-0 Pa. $8.95

THIRTY YEARS THAT SHOOK PHYSICS: The Story of Quantum Theory, George Gamow. Lucid, accessible introduction to influential theory of energy and matter. Careful explanations of Dirac's anti-particles, Bohr's model of the atom, much more. 12 plates. Numerous drawings. 240pp. 5⅜ × 8½. 24895-X Pa. $5.95

CHINESE DOMESTIC FURNITURE IN PHOTOGRAPHS AND MEASURED DRAWINGS, Gustav Ecke. A rare volume, now affordably priced for antique collectors, furniture buffs and art historians. Detailed review of styles ranging from early Shang to late Ming. Unabridged republication. 161 black-and-white drawings, photos. Total of 224pp. 8⅜ × 11¼. (Available in U.S. only) 25171-3 Pa. $13.95

VINCENT VAN GOGH: A Biography, Julius Meier-Graefe. Dynamic, penetrating study of artist's life, relationship with brother, Theo, painting techniques, travels, more. Readable, engrossing. 160pp. 5⅜ × 8½. (Available in U.S. only) 25253-1 Pa. $4.95

HOW TO WRITE, Gertrude Stein. Gertrude Stein claimed anyone could understand her unconventional writing—here are clues to help. Fascinating improvisations, language experiments, explanations illuminate Stein's craft and the art of writing. Total of 414pp. 4⅜ × 6⅜. 23144-5 Pa. $6.95

ADVENTURES AT SEA IN THE GREAT AGE OF SAIL: Five Firsthand Narratives, edited by Elliot Snow. Rare true accounts of exploration, whaling, shipwreck, fierce natives, trade, shipboard life, more. 33 illustrations. Introduction. 353pp. 5⅜ × 8½. 25177-2 Pa. $8.95

THE HERBAL OR GENERAL HISTORY OF PLANTS, John Gerard. Classic descriptions of about 2,850 plants—with over 2,700 illustrations—includes Latin and English names, physical descriptions, varieties, time and place of growth, more. 2,706 illustrations. xlv + 1,678pp. 8½ × 12¼. 23147-X Cloth. $75.00

DOROTHY AND THE WIZARD IN OZ, L. Frank Baum. Dorothy and the Wizard visit the center of the Earth, where people are vegetables, glass houses grow and Oz characters reappear. Classic sequel to *Wizard of Oz*. 256pp. 5⅜ × 8. 24714-7 Pa. $5.95

SONGS OF EXPERIENCE: Facsimile Reproduction with 26 Plates in Full Color, William Blake. This facsimile of Blake's original "Illuminated Book" reproduces 26 full-color plates from a rare 1826 edition. Includes "The Tyger," "London," "Holy Thursday," and other immortal poems. 26 color plates. Printed text of poems. 48pp. 5¼ × 7. 24636-1 Pa. $3.50

SONGS OF INNOCENCE, William Blake. The first and most popular of Blake's famous "Illuminated Books," in a facsimile edition reproducing all 31 brightly colored plates. Additional printed text of each poem. 64pp. 5¼ × 7. 22764-2 Pa. $3.50

PRECIOUS STONES, Max Bauer. Classic, thorough study of diamonds, rubies, emeralds, garnets, etc.: physical character, occurrence, properties, use, similar topics. 20 plates, 8 in color. 94 figures. 659pp. 6⅛ × 9¼. 21910-0, 21911-9 Pa., Two-vol. set $15.90

ENCYCLOPEDIA OF VICTORIAN NEEDLEWORK, S. F. A. Caulfeild and Blanche Saward. Full, precise descriptions of stitches, techniques for dozens of needlecrafts—most exhaustive reference of its kind. Over 800 figures. Total of 679pp. 8⅛ × 11. Two volumes. Vol. 1 22800-2 Pa. $11.95
Vol. 2 22801-0 Pa. $11.95

THE MARVELOUS LAND OF OZ, L. Frank Baum. Second Oz book, the Scarecrow and Tin Woodman are back with hero named Tip, Oz magic. 136 illustrations. 287pp. 5⅜ × 8½. 20692-0 Pa. $5.95

WILD FOWL DECOYS, Joel Barber. Basic book on the subject, by foremost authority and collector. Reveals history of decoy making and rigging, place in American culture, different kinds of decoys, how to make them, and how to use them. 140 plates. 156pp. 7⅞ × 10¾. 20011-6 Pa. $8.95

HISTORY OF LACE, Mrs. Bury Palliser. Definitive, profusely illustrated chronicle of lace from earliest times to late 19th century. Laces of Italy, Greece, England, France, Belgium, etc. Landmark of needlework scholarship. 266 illustrations. 672pp. 6⅛ × 9¼. 24742-2 Pa. $14.95

ILLUSTRATED GUIDE TO SHAKER FURNITURE, Robert Meader. All furniture and appurtenances, with much on unknown local styles. 235 photos. 146pp. 9 × 12. 22819-3 Pa. $8.95

WHALE SHIPS AND WHALING: A Pictorial Survey, George Francis Dow. Over 200 vintage engravings, drawings, photographs of barks, brigs, cutters, other vessels. Also harpoons, lances, whaling guns, many other artifacts. Comprehensive text by foremost authority. 207 black-and-white illustrations. 288pp. 6 × 9. 24808-9 Pa. $8.95

THE BERTRAMS, Anthony Trollope. Powerful portrayal of blind self-will and thwarted ambition includes one of Trollope's most heartrending love stories. 497pp. 5⅜ × 8½. 25119-5 Pa. $9.95

ADVENTURES WITH A HAND LENS, Richard Headstrom. Clearly written guide to observing and studying flowers and grasses, fish scales, moth and insect wings, egg cases, buds, feathers, seeds, leaf scars, moss, molds, ferns, common crystals, etc.—all with an ordinary, inexpensive magnifying glass. 209 exact line drawings aid in your discoveries. 220pp. 5⅜ × 8½. 23330-8 Pa. $4.95

RODIN ON ART AND ARTISTS, Auguste Rodin. Great sculptor's candid, wide-ranging comments on meaning of art; great artists; relation of sculpture to poetry, painting, music; philosophy of life, more. 76 superb black-and-white illustrations of Rodin's sculpture, drawings and prints. 119pp. 8⅜ × 11¼. 24487-3 Pa. $7.95

FIFTY CLASSIC FRENCH FILMS, 1912–1982: A Pictorial Record, Anthony Slide. Memorable stills from Grand Illusion, Beauty and the Beast, Hiroshima, Mon Amour, many more. Credits, plot synopses, reviews, etc. 160pp. 8¼ × 11. 25256-6 Pa. $11.95

THE PRINCIPLES OF PSYCHOLOGY, William James. Famous long course complete, unabridged. Stream of thought, time perception, memory, experimental methods; great work decades ahead of its time. 94 figures. 1,391pp. 5⅜ × 8½. 20381-6, 20382-4 Pa., Two-vol. set $23.90

BODIES IN A BOOKSHOP, R. T. Campbell. Challenging mystery of blackmail and murder with ingenious plot and superbly drawn characters. In the best tradition of British suspense fiction. 192pp. 5⅜ × 8½. 24720-1 Pa. $3.95

CALLAS: PORTRAIT OF A PRIMA DONNA, George Jellinek. Renowned commentator on the musical scene chronicles incredible career and life of the most controversial, fascinating, influential operatic personality of our time. 64 black-and-white photographs. 416pp. 5⅜ × 8¼. 25047-4 Pa. $8.95

GEOMETRY, RELATIVITY AND THE FOURTH DIMENSION, Rudolph Rucker. Exposition of fourth dimension, concepts of relativity as Flatland characters continue adventures. Popular, easily followed yet accurate, profound. 141 illustrations. 133pp. 5⅜ × 8½. 23400-2 Pa. $4.95

HOUSEHOLD STORIES BY THE BROTHERS GRIMM, with pictures by Walter Crane. 53 classic stories—Rumpelstiltskin, Rapunzel, Hansel and Gretel, the Fisherman and his Wife, Snow White, Tom Thumb, Sleeping Beauty, Cinderella, and so much more—lavishly illustrated with original 19th century drawings. 114 illustrations. x + 269pp. 5⅜ × 8½. 21080-4 Pa. $4.95

SUNDIALS, Albert Waugh. Far and away the best, most thorough coverage of ideas, mathematics concerned, types, construction, adjusting anywhere. Over 100 illustrations. 230pp. 5⅜ × 8½. 22947-5 Pa. $4.95

PICTURE HISTORY OF THE NORMANDIE: With 190 Illustrations, Frank O. Braynard. Full story of legendary French ocean liner: Art Deco interiors, design innovations, furnishings, celebrities, maiden voyage, tragic fire, much more. Extensive text. 144pp. 8⅜ × 11¾. 25257-4 Pa. $10.95

THE FIRST AMERICAN COOKBOOK: A Facsimile of "American Cookery," 1796, Amelia Simmons. Facsimile of the first American-written cookbook published in the United States contains authentic recipes for colonial favorites—pumpkin pudding, winter squash pudding, spruce beer, Indian slapjacks, and more. Introductory Essay and Glossary of colonial cooking terms. 80pp. 5⅜ × 8½. 24710-4 Pa. $3.50

101 PUZZLES IN THOUGHT AND LOGIC, C. R. Wylie, Jr. Solve murders and robberies, find out which fishermen are liars, how a blind man could possibly identify a color—purely by your own reasoning! 107pp. 5⅜ × 8½. 20367-0 Pa. $2.50

THE BOOK OF WORLD-FAMOUS MUSIC—CLASSICAL, POPULAR AND FOLK, James J. Fuld. Revised and enlarged republication of landmark work in musico-bibliography. Full information about nearly 1,000 songs and compositions including first lines of music and lyrics. New supplement. Index. 800pp. 5⅜ × 8¼. 24857-7 Pa. $15.95

ANTHROPOLOGY AND MODERN LIFE, Franz Boas. Great anthropologist's classic treatise on race and culture. Introduction by Ruth Bunzel. Only inexpensive paperback edition. 255pp. 5⅜ × 8½. 25245-0 Pa. $6.95

THE TALE OF PETER RABBIT, Beatrix Potter. The inimitable Peter's terrifying adventure in Mr. McGregor's garden, with all 27 wonderful, full-color Potter illustrations. 55pp. 4¼ × 5½. (Available in U.S. only) 22827-4 Pa. $1.75

THREE PROPHETIC SCIENCE FICTION NOVELS, H. G. Wells. *When the Sleeper Wakes, A Story of the Days to Come* and *The Time Machine* (full version). 335pp. 5⅜ × 8½. (Available in U.S. only) 20605-X Pa. $6.95

APICIUS COOKERY AND DINING IN IMPERIAL ROME, edited and translated by Joseph Dommers Vehling. Oldest known cookbook in existence offers readers a clear picture of what foods Romans ate, how they prepared them, etc. 49 illustrations. 301pp. 6⅛ × 9¼. 23563-7 Pa. $7.95

SHAKESPEARE LEXICON AND QUOTATION DICTIONARY, Alexander Schmidt. Full definitions, locations, shades of meaning of every word in plays and poems. More than 50,000 exact quotations. 1,485pp. 6½ × 9¼. 22726-X, 22727-8 Pa., Two-vol. set $29.90

THE WORLD'S GREAT SPEECHES, edited by Lewis Copeland and Lawrence W. Lamm. Vast collection of 278 speeches from Greeks to 1970. Powerful and effective models; unique look at history. 842pp. 5⅜ × 8½. 20468-5 Pa. $11.95

THE BLUE FAIRY BOOK, Andrew Lang. The first, most famous collection, with many familiar tales: Little Red Riding Hood, Aladdin and the Wonderful Lamp, Puss in Boots, Sleeping Beauty, Hansel and Gretel, Rumpelstiltskin; 37 in all. 138 illustrations. 390pp. 5⅜ × 8½. 21437-0 Pa. $6.95

THE STORY OF THE CHAMPIONS OF THE ROUND TABLE, Howard Pyle. Sir Launcelot, Sir Tristram and Sir Percival in spirited adventures of love and triumph retold in Pyle's inimitable style. 50 drawings, 31 full-page. xviii + 329pp. 6½ × 9¼. 21883-X Pa. $7.95

AUDUBON AND HIS JOURNALS, Maria Audubon. Unmatched two-volume portrait of the great artist, naturalist and author contains his journals, an excellent biography by his granddaughter, expert annotations by the noted ornithologist, Dr. Elliott Coues, and 37 superb illustrations. Total of 1,200pp. 5⅜ × 8.
Vol. I 25143-8 Pa. $8.95
Vol. II 25144-6 Pa. $8.95

GREAT DINOSAUR HUNTERS AND THEIR DISCOVERIES, Edwin H. Colbert. Fascinating, lavishly illustrated chronicle of dinosaur research, 1820's to 1960. Achievements of Cope, Marsh, Brown, Buckland, Mantell, Huxley, many others. 384pp. 5¼ × 8¼. 24701-5 Pa. $7.95

THE TASTEMAKERS, Russell Lynes. Informal, illustrated social history of American taste 1850's–1950's. First popularized categories Highbrow, Lowbrow, Middlebrow. 129 illustrations. New (1979) afterword. 384pp. 6 × 9.
23993-4 Pa. $8.95

DOUBLE CROSS PURPOSES, Ronald A. Knox. A treasure hunt in the Scottish Highlands, an old map, unidentified corpse, surprise discoveries keep reader guessing in this cleverly intricate tale of financial skullduggery. 2 black-and-white maps. 320pp. 5⅜ × 8½. (Available in U.S. only) 25032-6 Pa. $6.95

AUTHENTIC VICTORIAN DECORATION AND ORNAMENTATION IN FULL COLOR: 46 Plates from "Studies in Design," Christopher Dresser. Superb full-color lithographs reproduced from rare original portfolio of a major Victorian designer. 48pp. 9¼ × 12¼. 25083-0 Pa. $7.95

PRIMITIVE ART, Franz Boas. Remains the best text ever prepared on subject, thoroughly discussing Indian, African, Asian, Australian, and, especially, Northern American primitive art. Over 950 illustrations show ceramics, masks, totem poles, weapons, textiles, paintings, much more. 376pp. 5⅜ × 8. 20025-6 Pa. $7.95

SIDELIGHTS ON RELATIVITY, Albert Einstein. Unabridged republication of two lectures delivered by the great physicist in 1920–21. *Ether and Relativity* and *Geometry and Experience*. Elegant ideas in non-mathematical form, accessible to intelligent layman. vi + 56pp. 5⅜ × 8½. 24511-X Pa. $2.95

THE WIT AND HUMOR OF OSCAR WILDE, edited by Alvin Redman. More than 1,000 ripostes, paradoxes, wisecracks: Work is the curse of the drinking classes, I can resist everything except temptation, etc. 258pp. 5⅜ × 8½. 20602-5 Pa. $4.95

ADVENTURES WITH A MICROSCOPE, Richard Headstrom. 59 adventures with clothing fibers, protozoa, ferns and lichens, roots and leaves, much more. 142 illustrations. 232pp. 5⅜ × 8½. 23471-1 Pa. $3.95

PLANTS OF THE BIBLE, Harold N. Moldenke and Alma L. Moldenke. Standard reference to all 230 plants mentioned in Scriptures. Latin name, biblical reference, uses, modern identity, much more. Unsurpassed encyclopedic resource for scholars, botanists, nature lovers, students of Bible. Bibliography. Indexes. 123 black-and-white illustrations. 384pp. 6 × 9.   25069-5 Pa. $8.95

FAMOUS AMERICAN WOMEN: A Biographical Dictionary from Colonial Times to the Present, Robert McHenry, ed. From Pocahontas to Rosa Parks, 1,035 distinguished American women documented in separate biographical entries. Accurate, up-to-date data, numerous categories, spans 400 years. Indices. 493pp. 6½ × 9¼.   24523-3 Pa. $10.95

THE FABULOUS INTERIORS OF THE GREAT OCEAN LINERS IN HISTORIC PHOTOGRAPHS, William H. Miller, Jr. Some 200 superb photographs capture exquisite interiors of world's great "floating palaces"—1890's to 1980's: *Titanic, Ile de France, Queen Elizabeth, United States, Europa,* more. Approx. 200 black-and-white photographs. Captions. Text. Introduction. 160pp. 8⅜ × 11¼.
24756-2 Pa. $9.95

THE GREAT LUXURY LINERS, 1927–1954: A Photographic Record, William H. Miller, Jr. Nostalgic tribute to heyday of ocean liners. 186 photos of Ile de France, Normandie, Leviathan, Queen Elizabeth, United States, many others. Interior and exterior views. Introduction. Captions. 160pp. 9 × 12.
24056-8 Pa. $10.95

A NATURAL HISTORY OF THE DUCKS, John Charles Phillips. Great landmark of ornithology offers complete detailed coverage of nearly 200 species and subspecies of ducks: gadwall, sheldrake, merganser, pintail, many more. 74 full-color plates, 102 black-and-white. Bibliography. Total of 1,920pp. 8⅜ × 11¼.
25141-1, 25142-X Cloth. Two-vol. set $100.00

THE SEAWEED HANDBOOK: An Illustrated Guide to Seaweeds from North Carolina to Canada, Thomas F. Lee. Concise reference covers 78 species. Scientific and common names, habitat, distribution, more. Finding keys for easy identification. 224pp. 5⅜ × 8½.   25215-9 Pa. $6.95

THE TEN BOOKS OF ARCHITECTURE: The 1755 Leoni Edition, Leon Battista Alberti. Rare classic helped introduce the glories of ancient architecture to the Renaissance. 68 black-and-white plates. 336pp. 8⅜ × 11¼.   25239-6 Pa. $14.95

MISS MACKENZIE, Anthony Trollope. Minor masterpieces by Victorian master unmasks many truths about life in 19th-century England. First inexpensive edition in years. 392pp. 5⅜ × 8½.   25201-9 Pa. $8.95

THE RIME OF THE ANCIENT MARINER, Gustave Doré, Samuel Taylor Coleridge. Dramatic engravings considered by many to be his greatest work. The terrifying space of the open sea, the storms and whirlpools of an unknown ocean, the ice of Antarctica, more—all rendered in a powerful, chilling manner. Full text. 38 plates. 77pp. 9¼ × 12.   22305-1 Pa. $4.95

THE EXPEDITIONS OF ZEBULON MONTGOMERY PIKE, Zebulon Montgomery Pike. Fascinating first-hand accounts (1805-6) of exploration of Mississippi River, Indian wars, capture by Spanish dragoons, much more. 1,088pp. 5⅜ × 8½.   25254-X, 25255-8 Pa. Two-vol. set $25.90

A CONCISE HISTORY OF PHOTOGRAPHY: Third Revised Edition, Helmut Gernsheim. Best one-volume history—camera obscura, photochemistry, daguerreotypes, evolution of cameras, film, more. Also artistic aspects—landscape, portraits, fine art, etc. 281 black-and-white photographs. 26 in color. 176pp. 8⅜ × 11¼. 25128-4 Pa. $13.95

THE DORÉ BIBLE ILLUSTRATIONS, Gustave Doré. 241 detailed plates from the Bible: the Creation scenes, Adam and Eve, Flood, Babylon, battle sequences, life of Jesus, etc. Each plate is accompanied by the verses from the King James version of the Bible. 241pp. 9 × 12. 23004-X Pa. $9.95

HUGGER-MUGGER IN THE LOUVRE, Elliot Paul. Second Homer Evans mystery-comedy. Theft at the Louvre involves sleuth in hilarious, madcap caper. "A knockout."—Books. 336pp. 5⅜ × 8½. 25185-3 Pa. $5.95

FLATLAND, E. A. Abbott. Intriguing and enormously popular science-fiction classic explores the complexities of trying to survive as a two-dimensional being in a three-dimensional world. Amusingly illustrated by the author. 16 illustrations. 103pp. 5⅜ × 8½. 20001-9 Pa. $2.50

THE HISTORY OF THE LEWIS AND CLARK EXPEDITION, Meriwether Lewis and William Clark, edited by Elliott Coues. Classic edition of Lewis and Clark's day-by-day journals that later became the basis for U.S. claims to Oregon and the West. Accurate and invaluable geographical, botanical, biological, meteorological and anthropological material. Total of 1,508pp. 5⅜ × 8½.
21268-8, 21269-6, 21270-X Pa. Three-vol. set $26.85

LANGUAGE, TRUTH AND LOGIC, Alfred J. Ayer. Famous, clear introduction to Vienna, Cambridge schools of Logical Positivism. Role of philosophy, elimination of metaphysics, nature of analysis, etc. 160pp. 5⅜ × 8½. (Available in U.S. and Canada only) 20010-8 Pa. $3.95

MATHEMATICS FOR THE NONMATHEMATICIAN, Morris Kline. Detailed, college-level treatment of mathematics in cultural and historical context, with numerous exercises. For liberal arts students. Preface. Recommended Reading Lists. Tables. Index. Numerous black-and-white figures. xvi + 641pp. 5⅜ × 8½.
24823-2 Pa. $11.95

HANDBOOK OF PICTORIAL SYMBOLS, Rudolph Modley. 3,250 signs and symbols, many systems in full; official or heavy commercial use. Arranged by subject. Most in Pictorial Archive series. 143pp. 8⅛ × 11. 23357-X Pa. $6.95

INCIDENTS OF TRAVEL IN YUCATAN, John L. Stephens. Classic (1843) exploration of jungles of Yucatan, looking for evidences of Maya civilization. Travel adventures, Mexican and Indian culture, etc. Total of 669pp. 5⅜ × 8½.
20926-1, 20927-X Pa., Two-vol. set $11.90

DEGAS: An Intimate Portrait, Ambroise Vollard. Charming, anecdotal memoir by famous art dealer of one of the greatest 19th-century French painters. 14 black-and-white illustrations. Introduction by Harold L. Van Doren. 96pp. 5⅜ × 8½.
25131-4 Pa. $4.95

PERSONAL NARRATIVE OF A PILGRIMAGE TO ALMANDINAH AND MECCAH, Richard Burton. Great travel classic by remarkably colorful personality. Burton, disguised as a Moroccan, visited sacred shrines of Islam, narrowly escaping death. 47 illustrations. 959pp. 5⅜ × 8½. 21217-3, 21218-1 Pa., Two-vol. set $19.90

PHRASE AND WORD ORIGINS, A. H. Holt. Entertaining, reliable, modern study of more than 1,200 colorful words, phrases, origins and histories. Much unexpected information. 254pp. 5⅜ × 8½. 20758-7 Pa. $5.95

THE RED THUMB MARK, R. Austin Freeman. In this first Dr. Thorndyke case, the great scientific detective draws fascinating conclusions from the nature of a single fingerprint. Exciting story, authentic science. 320pp. 5⅜ × 8½. (Available in U.S. only) 25210-8 Pa. $6.95

AN EGYPTIAN HIEROGLYPHIC DICTIONARY, E. A. Wallis Budge. Monumental work containing about 25,000 words or terms that occur in texts ranging from 3000 B.C. to 600 A.D. Each entry consists of a transliteration of the word, the word in hieroglyphs, and the meaning in English. 1,314pp. 6⅜ × 10.
23615-3, 23616-1 Pa., Two-vol. set $31.90

THE COMPLEAT STRATEGYST: Being a Primer on the Theory of Games of Strategy, J. D. Williams. Highly entertaining classic describes, with many illustrated examples, how to select best strategies in conflict situations. Prefaces. Appendices. xvi + 268pp. 5⅜ × 8½. 25101-2 Pa. $5.95

THE ROAD TO OZ, L. Frank Baum. Dorothy meets the Shaggy Man, little Button-Bright and the Rainbow's beautiful daughter in this delightful trip to the magical Land of Oz. 272pp. 5⅜ × 8. 25208-6 Pa. $5.95

POINT AND LINE TO PLANE, Wassily Kandinsky. Seminal exposition of role of point, line, other elements in non-objective painting. Essential to understanding 20th-century art. 127 illustrations. 192pp. 6½ × 9¼. 23808-3 Pa. $5.95

LADY ANNA, Anthony Trollope. Moving chronicle of Countess Lovel's bitter struggle to win for herself and daughter Anna their rightful rank and fortune—perhaps at cost of sanity itself. 384pp. 5⅜ × 8½. 24669-8 Pa. $8.95

EGYPTIAN MAGIC, E. A. Wallis Budge. Sums up all that is known about magic in Ancient Egypt: the role of magic in controlling the gods, powerful amulets that warded off evil spirits, scarabs of immortality, use of wax images, formulas and spells, the secret name, much more. 253pp. 5⅜ × 8½. 22681-6 Pa. $4.50

THE DANCE OF SIVA, Ananda Coomaraswamy. Preeminent authority unfolds the vast metaphysic of India: the revelation of her art, conception of the universe, social organization, etc. 27 reproductions of art masterpieces. 192pp. 5⅜ × 8½.
24817-8 Pa. $5.95

CHRISTMAS CUSTOMS AND TRADITIONS, Clement A. Miles. Origin, evolution, significance of religious, secular practices. Caroling, gifts, yule logs, much more. Full, scholarly yet fascinating; non-sectarian. 400pp. 5⅜ × 8½.
23354-5 Pa. $6.95

THE HUMAN FIGURE IN MOTION, Eadweard Muybridge. More than 4,500 stopped-action photos, in action series, showing undraped men, women, children jumping, lying down, throwing, sitting, wrestling, carrying, etc. 390pp. 7⅞ × 10⅝.
20204-6 Cloth. $21.95

THE MAN WHO WAS THURSDAY, Gilbert Keith Chesterton. Witty, fast-paced novel about a club of anarchists in turn-of-the-century London. Brilliant social, religious, philosophical speculations. 128pp. 5⅜ × 8½. 25121-7 Pa. $3.95

A CEZANNE SKETCHBOOK: Figures, Portraits, Landscapes and Still Lifes, Paul Cezanne. Great artist experiments with tonal effects, light, mass, other qualities in over 100 drawings. A revealing view of developing master painter, precursor of Cubism. 102 black-and-white illustrations. 144pp. 8¾ × 6⅜. 24790-2 Pa. $5.95

AN ENCYCLOPEDIA OF BATTLES: Accounts of Over 1,560 Battles from 1479 B.C. to the Present, David Eggenberger. Presents essential details of every major battle in recorded history, from the first battle of Megiddo in 1479 B.C. to Grenada in 1984. List of Battle Maps. New Appendix covering the years 1967–1984. Index. 99 illustrations. 544pp. 6½ × 9¼. 24913-1 Pa. $14.95

AN ETYMOLOGICAL DICTIONARY OF MODERN ENGLISH, Ernest Weekley. Richest, fullest work, by foremost British lexicographer. Detailed word histories. Inexhaustible. Total of 856pp. 6½ × 9¼.
21873-2, 21874-0 Pa., Two-vol. set $17.00

WEBSTER'S AMERICAN MILITARY BIOGRAPHIES, edited by Robert McHenry. Over 1,000 figures who shaped 3 centuries of American military history. Detailed biographies of Nathan Hale, Douglas MacArthur, Mary Hallaren, others. Chronologies of engagements, more. Introduction. Addenda. 1,033 entries in alphabetical order. xi + 548pp. 6½ × 9¼. (Available in U.S. only)
24758-9 Pa. $13.95

LIFE IN ANCIENT EGYPT, Adolf Erman. Detailed older account, with much not in more recent books: domestic life, religion, magic, medicine, commerce, and whatever else needed for complete picture. Many illustrations. 597pp. 5⅜ × 8½.
22632-8 Pa. $8.95

HISTORIC COSTUME IN PICTURES, Braun & Schneider. Over 1,450 costumed figures shown, covering a wide variety of peoples: kings, emperors, nobles, priests, servants, soldiers, scholars, townsfolk, peasants, merchants, courtiers, cavaliers, and more. 256pp. 8⅜ × 11¼. 23150-X Pa. $9.95

THE NOTEBOOKS OF LEONARDO DA VINCI, edited by J. P. Richter. Extracts from manuscripts reveal great genius; on painting, sculpture, anatomy, sciences, geography, etc. Both Italian and English. 186 ms. pages reproduced, plus 500 additional drawings, including studies for *Last Supper, Sforza* monument, etc. 860pp. 7⅞ × 10¾. (Available in U.S. only) 22572-0, 22573-9 Pa., Two-vol. set $31.90

THE ART NOUVEAU STYLE BOOK OF ALPHONSE MUCHA: All 72 Plates from "Documents Decoratifs" in Original Color, Alphonse Mucha. Rare copyright-free design portfolio by high priest of Art Nouveau. Jewelry, wallpaper, stained glass, furniture, figure studies, plant and animal motifs, etc. Only complete one-volume edition. 80pp. 9⅜ × 12¼. 24044-4 Pa. $9.95

ANIMALS: 1,419 COPYRIGHT-FREE ILLUSTRATIONS OF MAMMALS, BIRDS, FISH, INSECTS, ETC., edited by Jim Harter. Clear wood engravings present, in extremely lifelike poses, over 1,000 species of animals. One of the most extensive pictorial sourcebooks of its kind. Captions. Index. 284pp. 9 × 12.
23766-4 Pa. $9.95

OBELISTS FLY HIGH, C. Daly King. Masterpiece of American detective fiction, long out of print, involves murder on a 1935 transcontinental flight—"a very thrilling story"—NY Times. Unabridged and unaltered republication of the edition published by William Collins Sons & Co. Ltd., London, 1935. 288pp. 5⅜ × 8½. (Available in U.S. only) 25036-9 Pa. $5.95

VICTORIAN AND EDWARDIAN FASHION: A Photographic Survey, Alison Gernsheim. First fashion history completely illustrated by contemporary photographs. Full text plus 235 photos, 1840–1914, in which many celebrities appear. 240pp. 6½ × 9¼. 24205-6 Pa. $6.95

THE ART OF THE FRENCH ILLUSTRATED BOOK, 1700–1914, Gordon N. Ray. Over 630 superb book illustrations by Fragonard, Delacroix, Daumier, Doré, Grandville, Manet, Mucha, Steinlen, Toulouse-Lautrec and many others. Preface. Introduction. 633 halftones. Indices of artists, authors & titles, binders and provenances. Appendices. Bibliography. 608pp. 8⅜ × 11¼. 25086-5 Pa. $24.95

THE WONDERFUL WIZARD OF OZ, L. Frank Baum. Facsimile in full color of America's finest children's classic. 143 illustrations by W. W. Denslow. 267pp. 5⅜ × 8½. 20691-2 Pa. $7.95

FRONTIERS OF MODERN PHYSICS: New Perspectives on Cosmology, Relativity, Black Holes and Extraterrestrial Intelligence, Tony Rothman, et al. For the intelligent layman. Subjects include: cosmological models of the universe; black holes; the neutrino; the search for extraterrestrial intelligence. Introduction. 46 black-and-white illustrations. 192pp. 5⅜ × 8½. 24587-X Pa. $7.95

THE FRIENDLY STARS, Martha Evans Martin & Donald Howard Menzel. Classic text marshalls the stars together in an engaging, non-technical survey, presenting them as sources of beauty in night sky. 23 illustrations. Foreword. 2 star charts. Index. 147pp. 5⅜ × 8½. 21099-5 Pa. $3.95

FADS AND FALLACIES IN THE NAME OF SCIENCE, Martin Gardner. Fair, witty appraisal of cranks, quacks, and quackeries of science and pseudoscience: hollow earth, Velikovsky, orgone energy, Dianetics, flying saucers, Bridey Murphy, food and medical fads, etc. Revised, expanded In the Name of Science. "A very able and even-tempered presentation."—The New Yorker. 363pp. 5⅜ × 8.
20394-8 Pa. $6.95

ANCIENT EGYPT: ITS CULTURE AND HISTORY, J. E Manchip White. From pre-dynastics through Ptolemies: society, history, political structure, religion, daily life, literature, cultural heritage. 48 plates. 217pp. 5⅜ × 8½. 22548-8 Pa. $5.95

SIR HARRY HOTSPUR OF HUMBLETHWAITE, Anthony Trollope. Incisive, unconventional psychological study of a conflict between a wealthy baronet, his idealistic daughter, and their scapegrace cousin. The 1870 novel in its first inexpensive edition in years. 250pp. 5⅜ × 8½. 24953-0 Pa. $5.95

LASERS AND HOLOGRAPHY, Winston E. Kock. Sound introduction to burgeoning field, expanded (1981) for second edition. Wave patterns, coherence, lasers, diffraction, zone plates, properties of holograms, recent advances. 84 illustrations. 160pp. 5⅜ × 8¼. (Except in United Kingdom) 24041-X Pa. $3.95

INTRODUCTION TO ARTIFICIAL INTELLIGENCE: SECOND, EN-LARGED EDITION, Philip C. Jackson, Jr. Comprehensive survey of artificial intelligence—the study of how machines (computers) can be made to act intelli-gently. Includes introductory and advanced material. Extensive notes updating the main text. 132 black-and-white illustrations. 512pp. 5⅜ × 8½. 24864-X Pa. $8.95

HISTORY OF INDIAN AND INDONESIAN ART, Ananda K. Coomaraswamy. Over 400 illustrations illuminate classic study of Indian art from earliest Harappa finds to early 20th century. Provides philosophical, religious and social insights. 304pp. 6⅜ × 9⅜. 25005-9 Pa. $9.95

THE GOLEM, Gustav Meyrink. Most famous supernatural novel in modern European literature, set in Ghetto of Old Prague around 1890. Compelling story of mystical experiences, strange transformations, profound terror. 13 black-and-white illustrations. 224pp. 5⅜ × 8½. (Available in U.S. only) 25025-3 Pa. $6.95

PICTORIAL ENCYCLOPEDIA OF HISTORIC ARCHITECTURAL PLANS, DETAILS AND ELEMENTS: With 1,880 Line Drawings of Arches, Domes, Doorways, Facades, Gables, Windows, etc., John Theodore Haneman. Sourcebook of inspiration for architects, designers, others. Bibliography. Captions. 141pp. 9 × 12. 24605-1 Pa. $7.95

BENCHLEY LOST AND FOUND, Robert Benchley. Finest humor from early 30's, about pet peeves, child psychologists, post office and others. Mostly unavailable elsewhere. 73 illustrations by Peter Arno and others. 183pp. 5⅜ × 8½. 22410-4 Pa. $4.95

ERTÉ GRAPHICS, Erté. Collection of striking color graphics: *Seasons, Alphabet, Numerals, Aces* and *Precious Stones*. 50 plates, including 4 on covers. 48pp. 9⅜ × 12¼. 23580-7 Pa. $7.95

THE JOURNAL OF HENRY D. THOREAU, edited by Bradford Torrey, F. H. Allen. Complete reprinting of 14 volumes, 1837–61, over two million words; the sourcebooks for *Walden*, etc. Definitive. All original sketches, plus 75 photographs. 1,804pp. 8½ × 12¼. 20312-3, 20313-1 Cloth., Two-vol. set $120.00

CASTLES: THEIR CONSTRUCTION AND HISTORY, Sidney Toy. Traces castle development from ancient roots. Nearly 200 photographs and drawings illustrate moats, keeps, baileys, many other features. Caernarvon, Dover Castles, Hadrian's Wall, Tower of London, dozens more. 256pp. 5⅜ × 8¼. 24898-4 Pa. $6.95

AMERICAN CLIPPER SHIPS: 1833–1858, Octavius T. Howe & Frederick C. Matthews. Fully-illustrated, encyclopedic review of 352 clipper ships from the period of America's greatest maritime supremacy. Introduction. 109 halftones. 5 black-and-white line illustrations. Index. Total of 928pp. 5⅜ × 8½.
25115-2, 25116-0 Pa., Two-vol. set $17.90

TOWARDS A NEW ARCHITECTURE, Le Corbusier. Pioneering manifesto by great architect, near legendary founder of "International School." Technical and aesthetic theories, views on industry, economics, relation of form to function, "mass-production spirit," much more. Profusely illustrated. Unabridged translation of 13th French edition. Introduction by Frederick Etchells. 320pp. 6⅛ × 9¼. (Available in U.S. only) 25023-7 Pa. $8.95

THE BOOK OF KELLS, edited by Blanche Cirker. Inexpensive collection of 32 full-color, full-page plates from the greatest illuminated manuscript of the Middle Ages, painstakingly reproduced from rare facsimile edition. Publisher's Note. Captions. 32pp. 9⅜ × 12¼. 24345-1 Pa. $4.95

BEST SCIENCE FICTION STORIES OF H. G. WELLS, H. G. Wells. Full novel *The Invisible Man*, plus 17 short stories: "The Crystal Egg," "Aepyornis Island," "The Strange Orchid," etc. 303pp. 5⅜ × 8½. (Available in U.S. only)
21531-8 Pa. $6.95

AMERICAN SAILING SHIPS: Their Plans and History, Charles G. Davis. Photos, construction details of schooners, frigates, clippers, other sailcraft of 18th to early 20th centuries—plus entertaining discourse on design, rigging, nautical lore, much more. 137 black-and-white illustrations. 240pp. 6⅛ × 9¼.
24658-2 Pa. $6.95

ENTERTAINING MATHEMATICAL PUZZLES, Martin Gardner. Selection of author's favorite conundrums involving arithmetic, money, speed, etc., with lively commentary. Complete solutions. 112pp. 5⅜ × 8½. 25211-6 Pa. $2.95

THE WILL TO BELIEVE, HUMAN IMMORTALITY, William James. Two books bound together. Effect of irrational on logical, and arguments for human immortality. 402pp. 5⅜ × 8½. 20291-7 Pa. $7.95

THE HAUNTED MONASTERY and THE CHINESE MAZE MURDERS, Robert Van Gulik. 2 full novels by Van Gulik continue adventures of Judge Dee and his companions. An evil Taoist monastery, seemingly supernatural events; overgrown topiary maze that hides strange crimes. Set in 7th-century China. 27 illustrations. 328pp. 5⅜ × 8½. 23502-5 Pa. $6.95

CELEBRATED CASES OF JUDGE DEE (DEE GOONG AN), translated by Robert Van Gulik. Authentic 18th-century Chinese detective novel; Dee and associates solve three interlocked cases. Led to Van Gulik's own stories with same characters. Extensive introduction. 9 illustrations. 237pp. 5⅜ × 8½.
23337-5 Pa. $4.95

Prices subject to change without notice.
Available at your book dealer or write for free catalog to Dept. GI, Dover Publications, Inc., 31 East 2nd St., Mineola, N.Y. 11501. Dover publishes more than 175 books each year on science, elementary and advanced mathematics, biology, music, art, literary history, social sciences and other areas.